Jurassic Coast Walks
DORSET & DEVON

Written by Nigel J. Clarke
Cover artwork by Anthony Clarke

Nigel J. Clarke Publications

www.nigelclarkepublications.co.uk
email: nigel@njcpublications.co.uk
Tel: 07808 321438

First edition 2006

ISBN 10 0-9552891-0-6
ISBN 13 978-0-9552891-0-1

Jurassic Coast Walks

The Walks

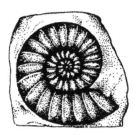

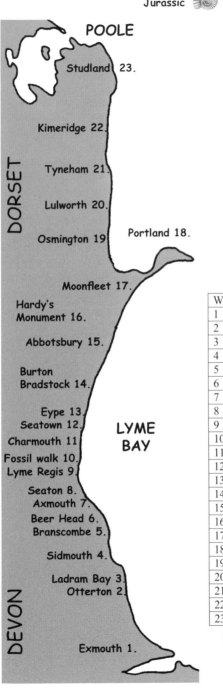

Jurassic Coast
Walks

POOLE

Studland 23.

Kimeridge 22.

Tyneham 21.

DORSET

Lulworth 20.

Osmington 19.   Portland 18.

Moonfleet 17.

Hardy's
Monument 16.

Abbotsbury 15.

Burton
Bradstock 14.

Eype 13.
Seatown 12.   LYME
Charmouth 11   BAY
Fossil walk 10.
Lyme Regis 9.

Seaton 8.
Axmouth 7.
Beer Head 6.
Branscombe 5.

Sidmouth 4.

Ladram Bay 3.
Otterton 2.

DEVON

Exmouth 1.

WALK	MILES	E	M	H	CHILD
1	6½	*			
2	5		*		*
3	3½		*		*
4	3	*			*
5	3½		*		*
6	2½	*			*
7	3½		*		
8	6			*	
9	2		*		*
10	1½	*			
11	4		*		
12	2½		*		
13	4½			*	
14	2	*			*
15	6			*	
16	3½		*		*
17	3	*			*
18	3	*			*
19	5		*		
20	8			*	
21	7½			*	
22	8½		*		
23	3½		*		

E = easy M = moderate H = hard
Walks 10 & 11 are tidal, so please
take care.

FOREWORD

I was going to dedicate this book to Spooks, the family dog, who seemed to think that writing a book about walks was the best idea since the invention of Bonio. But I'm afraid that while he enjoyed the walks, he thought the writing part too dull – though he seemed happy enough to accept his royalty rate in biscuits!

The walks described in this book are all in the West Dorset and East Devon area, going from Exmouth in the west, to Studland in the east. The lengths of the walks are all mostly no more than a morning or afternoon, though one or two are more vigorous and may take longer. Where beach walks are mentioned please check the times of the tides.

One drawback to walking in Dorset and Devon, especially for members of the Flat Earth Society are the hills; all seem steeper than the last, but the views form the top are a just reward, and at least you'll return fitter...

Many of the footpaths are extremely boggy and rutted, so I would recommend a stout pair of walking shoes; Wellington boots are a disaster for walking distances – even if the path were very muddy I would still wear hiking boots. Some of the coastal sections of the walks are very exposed, and while exhilarating at first, on windy days they soon become a misery, so always take the right clothing.

An ordnance survey map is not a necessity, but it is useful, especially on walks with stretches inland where footpaths can be harder to follow – taking a compass is also a good idea. All footpaths are open to the public, but please stick to the paths, do not trample crops, shut gates, and keep any dog on a lead when crossing fields containing livestock.

1. EXMOUTH - SANDY BAY - WEST DOWN - LITTLEHAM WALK

Walk Time: 2½ hours
Distance: 6½ miles
Walking: mostly easy

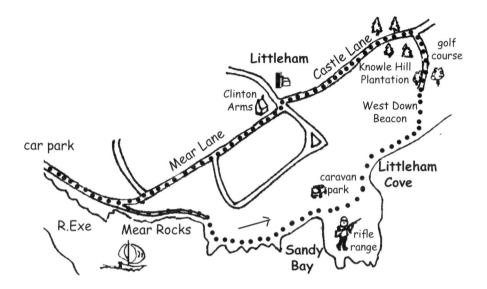

Exmouth is endowed with plenty of car parks. Try to leave your car in the large car park off Queen's Drive, which is the road that runs to the side of the river out to the headland. Park near the cafe, which is open all year, so that at the end of the excursion you can sit and ponder the walk over a cup of tea.

The walk starts from the car park and follows the road due east alongside the estuary of the River Exe. You have a choice; you can either walk along the beach, the pavement, or walk on the grass in the park.

Follow the road round to where it divides into two, at Fortes Foxholes Kiosk. One road carries along the sea front while the other bears off to the left; continue to the right of the toilets and kiosk and carry on up Foxholes Hill road. The coastal footpath bears off to the right a little way up this road. The path is signed and easy to follow.

As you walk up the footpath you look down on the estuary. The shipping channel is marked with red and green buoys that show the approach for the river. At the entrance to the river on the western side is a treacherous sand bar known as the Pole Sands, which over the years has caused a number of shipwrecks.

Until recently there was a commercial harbour at Exmouth but this has now closed. During the last century, sailing ships entered the Exe for the old commercial ports of Topsham and Exeter, where the export of wool was a major industry, but alas no more.

There is a sign just off the path on the right, which displays the distances; Sandy Bay is 1.5 miles and Budleigh Salterton is 4 miles. I have no doubt that in a couple of years time there will be a new law from the EU requiring all such signs to be in metric, and it will be illegal to read them in imperial; but kilometres do not have the same effect on feet as miles do.

One reason for Exmouth's popularity as a holiday resort is that it is one of the few places in Lyme Bay that you can build a sand castle - apart from the small sandy beach at Lyme Regis, the next sand is at Weymouth in Dorset. Over the years Exmouth has attracted notable worthies, among them Lady Nelson, wife of the hero of Trafalgar, who lived at a house called The Nob. Her grave lies in the churchyard at nearby Littleham, along with members of the Drake family. Lady Byron was also once a resident of the town.

The footpath runs up and on to the cliffs, with a splendid view of the estuary and beach below. To the right are Maer Rocks, and this area is a nature reserve, where numerous birds nest on the wooded cliffs. The headland at the end of the nature reserve is called Orcombe Point. The Exe estuary attracts thousands of migrating birds each year; among them are Brent Geese, Wigeon, Mallard, Teal, Scoters and Red Breasted Mergansers, but all this is further up the river from where we are.

You will notice that the sign on the left of the path specifically bans hang-gliding. So will all you walkers with a hang glider tucked in your sandwich box please refrain, though it seems cliff suicides are quite acceptable. We seem to live in an age where there is no viewing point safe from the local authority sign. They could have added, "Cliffs Are Dangerous, No Rockets, Do Not Approach Edge in Wet Weather", all obvious messages for the local sign industry. Carry along the footpath, which is easy to follow, carefully avoiding any illegal hang-gliders coming in to land.

The footpath leads out onto the area owned by the National Trust, marked by a pyramid stone marker. The route is easy to follow - just remember to have the sea on your right side. Follow the path towards Straight Point, which is the Royal Marine firing range. Hearing the sound of rapid machine-gun fire can be a bit unnerving, but at least you can be sure that you are walking in the right direction. Do not stray too close to the cliff edge unless you intend to try out a new quick-opening parachute; the drop is steep.

On your route you should pass a small corrugated cast-iron football stand, which is rusty with age. I can only presume this was built to give some protection to observers of the annual short-sighted Royal Marine rapid firing competition, when during World War II much of this area was used for training. The route leads on uphill towards the headland. Cross over the style through the gate. A thick hedge provides shelter from the prevailing southwest winds. Ahead in the distance you can see the rifle range, to the left is the massive Sandy Bay holiday park. The footpath goes down the hill towards the caravan holiday park.

The caravan park is enormous, and in the season caters for thousands of visitors, though off-season it is a sad, lonely place, where the inhabitants seem to have deserted the whole site like a land-bound Marie Celeste.

The footpath runs to left of the holiday park and the sea; a fence corrals you onto the path so you cannot become lost. The path emerges by the beach shop cafe, where you can obtain refreshment (though not in February). Below is a splendid beach; though do not swim too far out or you might get shot by an over-enthusiastic soldier. The footpath follows the perimeter fence of the firing range then crosses over a large car park, and continues to the left of the Calor gas storage area, up towards the hill. There is a sign for the coastal footpath. Follow the firing range fence to the left; carry on past the caravans and on towards the wooden chalets at the edge of the holiday park.

On the right is Littleham Cove, an attractive little beach. At the edge of the holiday park is a coastal footpath sign and direction for Budleigh Salterton, which is 1.5 miles. The footpath goes along the edge of Littleham Cove, up the hill to the top - West Down Beacon. There the .footpath turns off to the left away from the sea to Knowle Hill Plantations, and then the route heads back towards Exmouth.

The top of West Down Beacon is crowned with heather and gorse; hidden away is a large Golf course on the eastern side. The route leaves the fields and goes via a narrow path up, through the gorse to the summit of West Down Beacon. If you turn around and look due west you see the beautiful outline of the bay, and the red cliffs of south Devon.

Near the summit of West Down Beacon, the footpath comes to a junction that you need to take - the path off to the left that leads inland away from the sea, with the golf course on your right. The path goes past a water holding tank, fenced in with railings, to keep errant hang-gliding pilots out. The footpath emerges onto the golf course; and beware of the golfers, especially those about to hit the ball, as you will look pretty stupid wandering round Exmouth for the rest of the day with Dunlop stamped on your forehead!

The footpath is on the right and leads off the golf course towards the woods and onto a cart track, by the number eight tee. Follow the footpath to Knowle, carry on straight along this track till it eventually emerges onto a Tarmac country road called Castle Lane. At Castle Lane turn left (or due west) and follow the lane all the way to the village of Littleham.

At Littleham turn off and bear right past the Clinton Arms pub, down Maer Lane. The pub has an ornamental armoured car parked on the front lawn. This is certainly a vast improvement on ringing last orders and a considerable inducement to drink up. Follow Maer Lane all the way back down to Exmouth, and eventually you will come back to the mouth of the River Exe, and a short walk back to the starting point, and hope that the cafe is still open.

2. OTTERTON WALK
Walk Time: 2½ hours
Distance: 5 miles
Walking: easy, but steep in places

Park in the village of Otterton - normally there is plenty of room at the side of the village green - and walk back towards the main road, past Otterton Mill on your left. Go across the river by the first bridge, and take the path immediately on your left along the river, which is a public footpath signposted "Budleigh Salterton 2¾ miles".

The path is quite good, but made of earth, and could be squelchy when wet. The River Otter is on the left, quite wide, overgrown and slow-moving, with the possibility of seeing kingfishers, and in summer, martins nesting in holes in the red sandstone cliffs on the opposite bank a little further along. To the right across the field is the old Otterton station, which is now a private house, and beyond that is the Cleopatra's needle which marks the boundary of Bicton College of Agriculture.

After about 15 minutes, you reach a tricky metal gate (points for figuring out how it works first time), and immediately after that, go

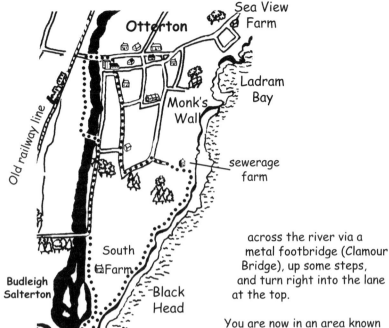

across the river via a metal footbridge (Clamour Bridge), up some steps, and turn right into the lane at the top.

You are now in an area known locally as "The Park", with lovely old trees, mostly chestnut, beech and oak. In autumn it's stiff with squirrels frantically stuffing nuts into holes in the ground. The river is now to your right, but mostly out of sight below you. Carry on along the lane until you meet another road. Follow it around to your left towards South Farm. Next to the farm entrance is the start of the coastal path to Ladram Bay, which is signposted. Take that path, with farmland to your left and the river and reed beds to your right. After five minutes, cross a narrow footbridge by a pond, and up a steep slope. At the top, take a detour down the gravel path on your right through pine trees to a hide that looks out over the river estuary at Budleigh Salterton. It's worth taking binoculars with you and spending some time here - at the very least you are almost certain to see a hunting kingfisher.

Back on the path, Budleigh Salterton with its red cliffs is now to your right across the river, and the sea is in front of you. Where the river meets Budleigh's beach, it has scoured out the back of the cliffs, and here the path swings to the left uphill and is signposted. Follow the path up onto the top of the cliffs, with the sea below you and great

9

views across Lyme Bay to the white cliffs of Beer. The edge of the cliff is not terribly well fenced, so you should keep an eye on dogs, small children and your granny.

If all is going to plan, you should now have the sea on your right, and farmland on your left. After the first five minutes, there is a steep climb, and then an easy walk for twenty minutes, mostly level or downhill.

The next (and last) very steep climb gives you brilliant views to nearby Ladram Bay, and beyond that the Picket Rocks, which you can stand and admire while having your heart attack. When the pains in your chest ease up, continue another 200 yards, over a stile and through a ruined building, which was an old wartime look-out post.

Carry on walking for another 10 minutes, and you'll reach a signposted track on your left, marked Otterton 1½ miles. Take the path, and turn inland. Over the next stile, turn left and then right beside a chain fence, and onto a stony track beside Otterton water treatment works.

At the end of this, bear left along another track signposted "Stantyway Road, Otterton 1¼ miles".

Through a gate (which will probably be open), and up a hill, where the track meets another. Follow it round to the right, ignoring the road on your left. Keep on the main track, and you should see a gate and another signpost in front of you, marked "Homedown, Otterton 1 mile". You are now on a properly made-up lane, with views of the big red cliff High Peak to your right.

You will soon reach some farm buildings, where you can either take a bridle path on your left back to the river Otter, or carry on along the lane. The bridle path can be overgrown, especially in summer.

If you follow the lane, it climbs steeply for five minutes, and shortly afterwards you reach the outskirts of Otterton. Carry on down the hill, and take the second turning on your left, Green Close, with the church and churchyard on your right. Note the griffin-shaped finial on the farm building in front of you. Follow the road round, passing the church of Saint Michael and All Angels on your right. At the bottom of the hill is the village green.

If you're in need of a coffee/tea transfusion now, you can turn left here, and the next large building is Otterton Mill, which is open daily all year round, and has a small restaurant, where you can make your recovery.

3. SIDMOUTH TO LADRAM BAY

Walk Time: 1¾ hours
Distance: 3½ miles
Walking: mostly easy, but steep in parts

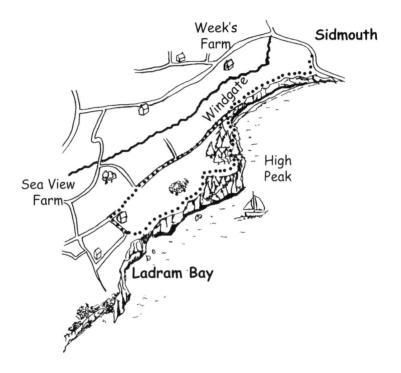

Start by driving to the large free car park right at the top of Peak Hill - the cliff on the Western side of Sidmouth - reached on the Sidmouth to Otterton road.

Across the road, opposite the entrance to the car park, there is a kissing gate signposted "Public Footpath Link to Coast Path", and leading to a clearly defined path across a grassy field. Take this path, walking due south towards the top of the cliff. Here, turn to your right and follow the path as it runs along the cliff top. The big red cliff to your left and in front of you is High Peak.

After two stiles, the track leads gently up towards the woods covering the back of High Peak. Over a third style, and you enter the woods, and almost immediately come to a seat with wonderful views. As your body has probably only just twigged that this is not a casual stroll

11

down to the corner shop, it's a good spot to stop and let it get over the shock. The cliff to your left is Peak Hill, stretching away till it ends at Jacob's Ladder, which is the white construction running from the cliff top to beach. This is the "new" ladder; the steeper and more lethal stone original is just out of sight round the corner of the cliffs. Beyond Jacob's Ladder is Sidmouth, and where the cliffs turn from blood-red to white, Beer Head.

When you feel strong enough, carry on along the path. Soon you'll reach a three-armed signpost; follow the arm that points up to your left and is marked "Ladram ¾ mile Coast Path", through a gate and into a plantation of well-grown conifers. This is not the usual grim, gloomy wood that you generally associate with fir trees; the trees are well spaced with plenty of elder, ferns and foxgloves.

If you feel really keen and determined there are two or three well-defined and very steep tracks on your left that will take you right to the top of High Peak. You'll know when you find the summit as it is marked by an Ordinance Survey beacon, right on the edge. The views are great, but it can be a real scramble to reach, and probably not worth the extra effort unless you have mountain goat in your genes.

Rejoin the path and carry on through the woods, out into the open, and downhill all the way to Ladram Bay. Over one more stile, and across a field with lovely views of the rock formations (and the caravan site!). If you have binoculars with you, there are plenty of places to stop and bird-watch, looking for cormorants, seagulls nesting, puffins, sea lions, mermaids...

At the bottom of the field, hop over the stile and get your best view yet of the cliffs and rock stacks. Follow the grass right down to the bottom, keeping the Three Rocks Inn (that's the big brown thing you thought was a power station) on your right. When you run out of grass and power station, turn to the right onto a Tarmac path beside a pretty thatched cottage. From here you can take a detour down onto the beach, but be warned that dogs are not allowed.

Past the thatched cottage and the Marine Awareness Centre on your right, and before you reach the cafe, you will see a signpost in front of you, with one arm (marked with a black circle) indicating the start of a lane to the right. As well as the cafe, there are also public loos, telephones and a shop here - handy if you forgot to pack the sandwiches, or decide to puddle about on the beach and need extra supplies.

Take the indicated lane, which will lead you gently uphill away from the caravans, until you reach Sea View Farm. Beyond the farm, turn right into a lane signposted "Public right of way Bar's Lane". This is a wide farm track, passing through fields well away from traffic and noise. After about ten minutes walking, the lane leads you back into the woods below High Peak, with farmland to your left and woods to your right. Here it can get very muddy - not the place to wear high heels, especially if you're a chap. Eventually you arrive back at the three-armed post where you branched into the woods on your outward journey. Carry straight on, the way indicated "Coast path Sidmouth 1½ miles", retracing your steps back to your car.

4. SIDMOUTH - SALCOMBE HILL WALK

Walk Time: 1½ hours
Distance: 3 miles
Walking: easy

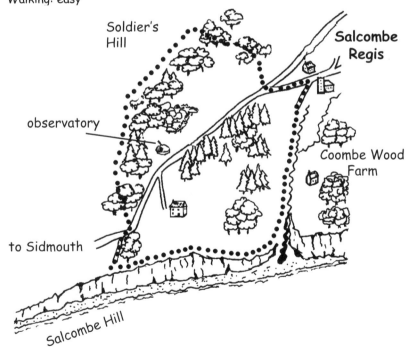

Start the walk at the Salcombe Hill car park. This is a free car park, owned by the National Trust, and located the top of Salcombe Hill - the cliff on the eastern side of the town. (To find it, follow the signs for the Norman Lockyer Observatory, which is opposite the car park.)

There is a gate and driveway to a house called "Southdown" next to the car park, signposted "Salcombe Hill Cliff and link to Coast Path". Take this driveway, which is also a public right of way, turning to your left, towards the sea.

Just before you reach the house, you will see a gate in front of you, and the path beyond. Go through the gate, and straight on, ignoring other paths to the right and left. Below to your right lies Sidmouth, and beyond that the big red cliffs, Peak Hill and High Peak, and below them the distinctive rock outcrops of Lade's Foot and Ladram Bay. At the end of this path, turn left through a gate, onto the path signposted "Coast Path, Salcombe Mouth ½ mile". The concrete post on the bank beside you marks the site of one of the ancient signal beacons, used to warn of impending disaster in the centuries before modern communications. Through the gate, you are on the land of South Combe Farm, which has been given by its owner as a permanent open space. Follow the path along the top of the cliff, with the sea on your right, and fabulous views towards Beer Head, Golden Cap, and on a rain free day, Portland Bill. In summer, you are certain to hear skylarks singing, and in autumn the blackberries on the cliff-edge are lush.

Through the next gate, carry on down the path as far as the large stone (the Frogstone) you'll see to the left. Unless you want to do a mountain-goat impersonation, turn left at the stone, and take the path that leads directly away from the sea inland, with the valley of Salcombe Regis below to your right. At the end of the first field, go through the five-bar gate, and carry on along the path at the edge of the field, with trees to your right, through another five-bar gate and onto a farm track, which takes you down into woods. Where the track meets another track coming from the right, you will see a kissing-gate straight in front of you. Go through this gate into the woods.

You immediately come to a signpost; take the path signposted "128 Public Footpath" straight in front of you - don't go to either the right or left. This path takes you into a dense forest of mature fir trees. Go straight on ignoring the path for Soldiers Hill. It can be a bit boggy underfoot here, but passable, and in summer the woods are cool and dark and filled with bird song.

Once out of the woods, you will reach a gate onto the road. (Although this is just a minor road, locals tend to whiz along it because it's so straight, so be careful, especially if you have children or animals with you.) Turn right on the road, and walk about twenty yards, where you will see a footpath on the other side of the road signposted "Public Bridleway - Milltown Lane". Take this track. You should now be able to see the four domes of the Norman Lockyer Observatory across the field to the left. Where the path splits, ignore the path to Soldiers Hill, and carry on the smaller path straight in front of you, which leads you gently downhill into a wood of mixed deciduous trees, quite different from the wood you have just left. It is worth walking quietly here, and peeping over the high bank to your right and down into the woods below, as I have often managed to see deer and fox here.

You will soon come to a post with a yellow arrow pointing down over what is known as Forty Nine Steps, and a blue arrow pointing straight ahead. Follow the blue arrow. Through another gate, and you are now entering an area that was once a private garden many years ago, complete with parrots and monkeys. You can still see the enormous rhododendrons, and carpets of bluebells in spring. Over some dinky footbridges, which save you from a particularly swampy part of the path, and back up onto the road.

Turn right, and walk downhill a few yards, to the upward-pointing sign "Public Footpath" on the opposite side. This path is quite steep, and tricky in the wet. If it's too nasty, just walk uphill on the road instead, which will take you back to the car park. If you take the footpath, you will puff up between some lovely elderly pine trees, emerging with the house called Southdown right in front of you. Turn left, back along the driveway to the car park.

You could combine your walk with a visit to the Norman Lockyer Observatory, just across the road, built by Sir Norman Lockyer, who was famous for his discovery of helium. The grounds are open to the public all year round, and the domes and brand-new planetarium are open at various times during the year. Telephone the Sidmouth Tourist Information Centre or Library to check on opening times.

5. BRANSCOMBE WALK

Walk Time: 1¾ hours
Distance: 3½ miles
Walking: mostly easy, though the first part is very steep

This historic and attractive village nestles into the most westerly outcrop of England's chalk cliffs. Sidmouth is 3½ miles to the west, and Seaton 3 miles to the east.

Take the Branscombe turn-off from the A3052 (Lyme Regis to Exeter road). The lane is narrow and twisting; follow the sign for the beach, and park in the car park to the front of the restaurant, The Sea Shanty - an ideal place for lunch or breakfast.

Walk up the hill behind the restaurant, and take the second path, marked "Coast Path - Weston Mouth", through the gate towards the old coastguard cottages now converted into a single dwelling. Dogs should be kept on a lead while crossing the first two fields as they often have sheep and lambs in spring.

Follow the footpath up across the second field and cross the stile onto the wind-swept expanse of West Cliff. This first stage of the walk is quite steep, and can be very unpleasant going in wet weather. Behind and to the left in the valley is the village of Branscombe, hiding from the sea and protected from the winter gales. Hooken Cliffs are opposite - the scene of a major landslide in 1790, when 10 acres of land slipped and plunged 200ft into the sea. The coastline here is subject to continuous erosion and 3 metres are lost on average each century.

The footpath continues westwards along the back of the cliffs, over a double stile where the path becomes an easily-followed cart track, though on a hot summer's day it is nicer to benefit from the sea breeze nearer the cliff edge. The track runs through the lightly wooded hills and is heavily rutted and muddy after rain. The local woodland contains a variety of flowers including daffodils, bluebells, red campion and scabious; more pungent is the aromatic smell of wild garlic in spring.

The track passes a young plantation on the side of the hill. Follow the path until you reach a post with a yellow arrow pointing to the right and marked "Street". Leave the track here, but do not follow the direction of the arrow; instead, turn hard right and follow the field downhill, with scrub to your left and woods to your right. Head for the bottom left of the field, where you will find a stile. Over this and onto a path that descends through the woods to the village, with its picturesque thatched cottages and well-maintained gardens. The footpath emerges from the trees, over another stile, and into a steep-sided field.

Opposite you, across the other side of the valley is the old Methodist Chapel. Head for this building as you scrabble about on the sheep tracks down over the field, and you will reach the stile out onto the road.

Turn right, and follow the road towards the sea and car park. On the way you will pass the church of St. Winifred's, which is worth a detour to visit. Christianity came to Branscombe in about 400 AD, and an earlier Saxon church, also dedicated to St. Winifred (a Welsh virgin martyr) existed on the site. The present church dates in part from about 1130 AD, with a fine Norman tower. The chancel of the church, built in the 14th century, has a wagon roof made from over 60 metres of oak beams, and there is also an interesting three-tier pulpit. The house opposite, called "Church Living", is 13th century and was the former curate's home, and is now a private residence.

Further along the street, at the bottom of the hill, the Old Bakery is now a tearoom, and open all year round. On the other side of the road is the thatched blacksmith's forge.

Next to the blacksmith's is the Village Hall. Opposite this, on your right, take the lane marked "Linked public footpath - Branscombe Mouth". Pass Manor Mill on your right, and carry on, following the stream and signs for Branscombe Mouth, until you eventually come back to the car park next to the beach.

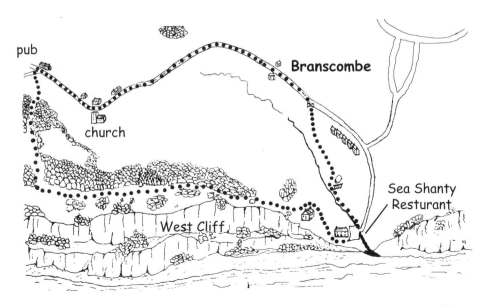

6. BEER HEAD WALK
Walk Time: 1 hour 20 minutes
Distance: 2½ miles
Walking: mostly easy

Drive down through the old village of Beer, once a haunt of smugglers, and one of the prettiest villages in Devon. The name comes from the Old English word beare, meaning a grove.

The main high street leads down to the cove; you follow the road past the shops and pubs and bear off to the right up the lane with the sea on your left. Follow the lane up the hill till you arrive at the car park, which is located just short of the large caravan site.

The walk follows the coastal footpath, which makes its way along the edge of the cliffs. The footpath is well signed. The path follows the coastline westward towards Branscombe, which is about 2 miles distant. The route is well used and easy to follow. Cross the field and go through the gate. If you care to stop and look behind towards the east you will see the small town of Seaton, and at the far end the mouth of the River Axe, above which is the golf club, and the start of the large nature

Car Park

Caravan Site

South Down Farm

Arratt's Hill

Old Coastguard Look Out

Hooken Beach

Beer Head

reserve that runs between Seaton and Lyme Regis. It was part of this coastal stretch where a major landslide occurred on Christmas Eve 1839, when 20 acres of land sank into a chasm. The pressure of the slip caused the seabed to rise up, and a reef was pushed up off shore. The reef has long since disappeared, eroded by the sea.

Further along the coast of Lyme Bay is Golden Cap, the distinct cliff that is aptly named with its topping of yellows sands. Golden Cap is the highest point along the south coast rising 617 ft above sea level. Along from Golden Cap is the start of the Chesil Beach which curves round to the unmistakable hump of Portland Bill, on which at night you can see the lighthouse twinkling. I am of course describing all these features on a sunny and clear day, and for many these views will be lost in the sea mists... back to the footpath!

Carry on along the coastal footpath. The steep cliffs ahead on the left are know as "The Hall", which seems a strange name, but I suppose you could hardly call them "The Cliffs"! At the foot of the cliffs is Pound's Pool Beach. The footpath continues along towards Beer Head. It is this headland that shelters Beer from the prevailing south west winds and provides one of the few safe anchorage's along this coast in a south west gale. In 1995 a parachutist tried to jump from the top of Beer head but on his descent his chute became snagged on the rock face and he slammed into the cliff, breaking his leg. The Beer coastguard team were able to free the man and he eventually recovered from the accident.

Above the cliff, perched on the edge, is an old Coastguard lookout tower; it is towards these buildings we are heading. Along the footpath there is a stile to the left that takes a route down the cliffs and onto the beach via an area called Under Hooken. Carry on past this diversion and over the next stile, and on towards the Coastguard lookout, which has now been converted into a holiday cottage. It was originally built as a Lloyds of London signalling station, one of many along the coast that relayed the movement and arrival of shipping from ports along the south coast to London, by means of signalling panels. The Coastguard eventually took over the station and built the cottages to the side for the staff. During the war the station was also used as an observatory and early warning lookout for planes and German shipping movements.

The track back to the car runs from the corner of the cottage due east away from the cliffs. The cart track is well worn and easy to follow, and exits the field through the gate. Follow the cart track all the way to a Tarmac lane, where you should be able to see the caravan park; below is the car park and the starting point of this walk. You can either go back to the car or down into the village for food and refreshment.

7. AXMOUTH WALK
Walk Time: 1½ hours
Distance: 3½ miles
Walking: vigorous, with steep and muddy parts

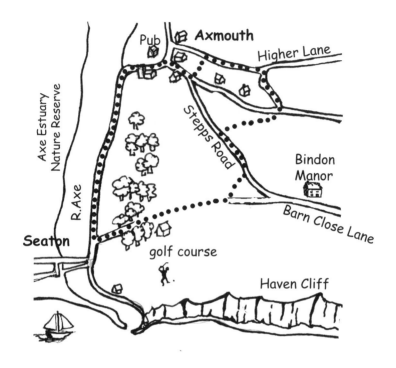

Axmouth is a pretty village on the eastern edge of Devon. The cottages snuggle close to the eastern banks of the River Axe. Historically once an important port, the river both brought wealth and removed it. We know from records that at one time vessels could sail up to the village to load and unload their cargoes. The port fell into decline due to rock falls that narrowed the entrance into the river and caused the channels to silt up, and in the nineteenth century a bridge was built down-river nearer the sea, denying access for any masted ship.

The best place to park is at the Harbour Inn, but only park here if you are to avail yourself of the Inn's splendid food and drink. This old pub also has a pleasant beer garden. There are plenty of side roads that can be parked in, Axmouth being one of the few places along the coast where the local authorities have not corralled cars into municipal car parks with the use of yellow lines!

Our route follows the estuary down to the sea. The village has many attractive cottages, and a traditional village school. On your left you will pass the Parish Church of St Michael, which has some striking stone gargoyles hanging from the tower. The church is thought to date back to the Anglo-Saxon period. Follow the footpath out of the village and past the old slipway and picnic site. From this recreation area there is a great view of the estuary.

The River Axe and its estuary fill the whole valley, and the narrowing of the river mouth has created salt marshes, some of which were reclaimed in the nineteenth century by drainage and dykes to create new pasture. The tramline runs on top of the bank on the western side of the estuary. The tram station is near the sea front at Seaton, and the line follows the Axe all the way to Colyton.

To the left is the town of Seaton, with it rash of bungalows spreading inland. If you look down the valley towards the sea you will see the first of two bridges. The nearest is a recent construction and now takes all the traffic. The older bridge was built in the nineteenth century and is a listed monument, as it's said to be one of the first bridges in England to be built out of concrete. I will leave you to judge the architectural merits of this structure, which to me has all the appeal of bag of cement left too long in the rain.

Follow the footpath down the valley towards the bridges. The road is very noisy, which is pity as it is hard to hear the numerous cries of the birds that nest and feed on this important ornithological site. The mud flats exposed at low tide attract numerous feeders. Among the birds that can be seen are: Red Shank, Shell Duck, Wigeon, Teal, Oyster Catcher, Lapwing, Ringed Plover, Curlew, Cormorants, Grebes, Kingfishers and Herons. The river also has a diverse fish stock and in recent years the gravel beds have been replenished further up-stream, to encourage larger numbers of salmon, which have declined at an alarming rate during the last twenty years.

Just before you get to the bridge you will see a sign for "Axe Valley Golf Club" and another sign for the coastal footpath (Lyme Regis $7\frac{1}{2}$ miles). Follow this sign, which points to the steep lane up the hill on the left hand side. For those in mind of a detour, carry on down the road to the harbour at Axmouth, and follow the track on the left through the gate down to the sea. The harbour is crammed with sailing boats, and it is surprising how narrow the entrance to the sea is from the river. At low water it would seem impossible that anyone could use this harbour.

The route ascends the hill and we are at last away from the noise of the road and the traffic. Although the estuary is a pleasant walk, it is probably best done early in the morning when there are fewer vehicles about. The walk is now from near sea level up the side of the valley to about 110m above sea level. At a pleasant stroll - you should take about 30 minutes from the start of the walk.

The coastal hedgerows in Devon are lush and green with many ferns growing at the base. There is one called "Mother's Tongue" which grows at the base of the hedge. I am always amazed at how some one came up with the folk names of plants, Dragon Tongue perhaps, but not Mother's Tongue! Follow the lane up towards the Axmouth Golf Club, past the houses on the right, with beautiful terraced gardens. The footpath passes to the left of the Golf Club out onto the course. The path is well marked, but do watch out for the golfers, especially angry ones who have miss-hit the ball and shot it down the valley towards the sea. The footpath crosses the course and heads towards a lane that emerges from the hedge to the top of the hill. To the left of the lane entrance is a wooden shed.

At the lane entrance, stop, turn round and try to regain any composure that breathing like an ox short of oxygen can bring. The view is stunning. Below is the town of Seaton, and in the distance are the white cliffs of Beer Head and the small smuggling village of Beer. You should now be about 40 to 50 minutes into the walk, and you will no doubt be pleased to know that you have done the steepest part.

Walk on up the track, known as Barn Close Lane. After a short walk you will come to a footpath junction; on the right is the Coastal Footpath to Lyme Regis, and on the left is the signed footpath for Axmouth, (1/2 mile). It is the left hand footpath that we want. This is the turning point in the walk and the leg back to Axmouth begins. From the top of the hill inland you can see the television mast at Stockland, which I will call 12 o' clock, at 9.30 is the old water-cooling tower now converted into a house, perched on the hill overlooking Seaton, and out to sea are the white cliffs of Beer.

The footpath runs downhill and across the middle of the field, and eventually emerges over a stile onto a Tarmac lane called Steeps Road. Follow the lane down the hill past Parsonage Barn on the right and a chalet house called Hawk Lodge on the left. The footpath we need is opposite this house, after the farm buildings.

The path here is very muddy, though someone has kindly left some planks to walk on. Follow the footpath to the right and towards the lane that can be seen ahead. The footpath crosses the second field diagonally towards the first house built on the left hand side of the road in the top left corner. Climb over the stile here to get into the lane.

Once in the lane, turn right and walk up the hill past the terraced cottages and towards the entrance of Bindon Manor. The driveway to the Manor is on the right but we need to take the bridle way on the left that curls round the back of the cottage (Gate Keepers Cottage). The route is signed. The bridle path ascends the hill and emerges after a barn on the right hand side onto Higher Lane. Turn left and follow the lane down the hill, but look out for the signed footpath on the left, which is at the end of the terraced cottage gardens. Follow this path down to the lower lane, where at the bottom you turn right and after 5 minutes emerge back at your starting point. The next step is food and a well-deserved drink.

8. THE CLIFF WALK FROM LYME REGIS TO SEATON

Walk time: $3\frac{1}{2}$ - 4 hours
Distance: 6 miles
Walking: hard

The walk starts from Holmbush car park, which is located at the top of the town on the Seaton road. The path onto the cliffs is in the right-hand corner of the car park and is marked by a sign outlining the route of the Southwest coastal walk of which this walk is part. The track goes past the houses and onto the start of Ware Cliffs. The footpath runs parallel to the sea and to the left of the old town reservoir, of which only the earth embankments remain.

There is a delightful view of the Cobb below. It was from these cliffs during the English Civil War that the Royalist forces fired on the Parliamentary-held Cobb sinking several ships. Stonebarrow and Golden Cap can also be seen, as can Portland Bill on a clear day.

Follow the footpath up towards the bungalow, which nestles into the cliffs, pass through the gate and turn left onto the cart track that leads down to Underhill Farm. To the right of the track is the start of the heavily wooded nature reserve. At Underhill Farm the footpath begins. A conveniently placed sign and map of the route mark the start of the path. Underhill Farm was one of several local locations used in the filming of the French Lieutenant's Woman, the cinematic adaptation of John Fowles' locally based novel.

The first section of the path can be extremely boggy, especially after heavy rain, boots and a stout stick are a necessity at such times. In spring the sides of the footpath are scattered with wild primroses and later, bluebells. In the late summer the gorse and bracken are easily ignited so care should be taken with matches and cigarettes.

One of my favourite spots of the walk is soon reached. A large, heavily shaded pond that seems to attract an abundance of birds, heard only when the walker is silent. It's surprising how much noise we tend to create when walking, and how completely oblivious we are to the animal and bird-life around us. It is worth pausing by these ponds to listen in quietness; you will be surprised by the number of bird sounds, and if you are very lucky you may even hear or see some of the larger animals that live in the reserve such as deer, fox and badgers, though such animals are more easily seen on dawn walks.

After the ponds the footpath passes some old ivy clad walls, long since fallen into ruin. A local landowner built the walls in the last century to keep trespassers out, though in his enthusiasm to preserve his privacy he also blocked off a public right of way, but after a prolonged series of legal battles people were once more allowed to use the footpath.

Much of the land in this stretch

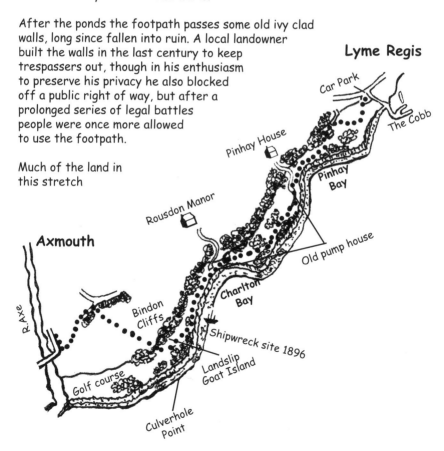

Lyme Regis

Car Park

The Cobb

Pinhay House

Pinhay Bay

Rousdon Manor

Old pump house

Axmouth

R. Axe

Bindon Cliffs

Charlton Bay

Shipwreck site 1896

Golf course

Landslip Goat Island

Culverhole Point

of the walk is moving and slipping towards the sea and it is dangerous to wander off the path, especially to the sea side. The footpath eventually emerges onto a rough track, built by the Water Board for the maintenance of their pumping station at Pinhay Bay. The walking is easier and less muddy than the previous section of footpath. The track eventually reaches the green painted pump house, and a convenient turn round point for those either too tired or lacking the time to carry on to Seaton.

PINHAY PUMP STATION, DOWNLANDS TO SEATON
The cliff top track is well signposted and runs up the hill to the side of the pump station and then turns left running parallel to the sea and towards the west. A short walk beyond the pump station, the force of earth movement has pulled the roots of large trees out of the ground, tilting the land nearly 2ft over a 12 month period, the footpath has also been disturbed. I congratulate the people who regularly maintain the path and build new steps as required.

Depending on the time of year, a pungent smell permeates through the air; have no fear, you are not about to stumble on a remote part of the Wimpy Empire, the plant responsible is the wild garlic that grows in profusion all along the side of this stretch of the path.

The footpath carries on up and down - though the ups seem to come quicker than the downs - eventually reaching a clearing and spring at Charton Bay. The water has been channelled into a series of pools, an ideal place to wash muddy shoes and children; in spring the pools contain frogspawn and later in the year tadpoles. In the surrounding vegetation you will find adders and grass snakes, though the adder is found in greater numbers and some large specimens have been found in recent years, but are such shy and timid creatures that few are seen by walkers.

The footpath carries on across the bridge (the track on the right goes on up to Rousdon Estate and eventually out onto the main road at Rousdon), and turns off to the left, then to the right at the second intersection of paths.

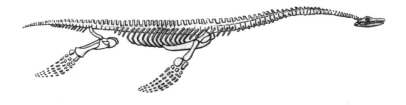

Slowly the path ascends, eventually reaching Bindon Cliffs, the scene of the most spectacular slip in 1839. The slip occurred shortly before Christmas of that year after an exceptionally wet autumn. Fifteen acres of farmland slipped down into a chasm and remained intact, with hedges and growing cornfields. The pressure of the slip uplifted a reef a quarter of a mile off shore, 40ft high and nearly a mile in length. At the time, the slip attracted a great deal of publicity, though little of the resulting chasm can now be seen, and the sea has long since destroyed the reef. There is a picture of the slip in the Harbour Inn at Axmouth (a refreshing stop to eat and drink after the walk), which was drawn at the time.

The footpath ascends the cliffs and eventually comes out on to the Downlands, an area typical of Dorset and Devon's sheep farming land. You cross the stile and follow the path along the field. In the second field, cross diagonally to the gate in the far corner and follow the hedge on the left of the gate onto the farm track. At the end of the track is the golf course; walk straight on to the golf club and following the Tarmac road down to the river. There is a bus that runs along the coast back to Lyme Regis.

9. LYME REGIS WARE CLIFF WALK
Walk time: 1 hour
Distance: 2 miles
Walking: steep and can be muddy and slippery in places

The walk begins at Lyme Regis' famous harbour, the Cobb.

The Royal Standard pub is about 400 years old, with timbers in the bar from old sailing ships, and a pleasant sheltered beer garden. It makes a good start for the walk. From the front door, turn left along Marine Parade towards the square. On your right are the old bonded warehouses of the harbour, now converted into flats. The house straight ahead is the old harbourmaster's house. Carry on into the main square, and past the lifeboat station and the entrance to the Cobb. Turn right along the road, which runs due, west parallel to the sea. The stony beach to the left is called Monmouth Beach, and it was here in 1685 that the Duke of Monmouth landed in his ill-fated attempt to gain the English throne from James II. Monmouth was subsequently defeated at the battle of Sedgemoor, and beheaded at the Tower of London. Some of his supporters were hung from gibbets erected on the beach at Lyme.

Carry on up the road for about 50 yards, past the bowling club green, and on your left is the marker for the coastal footpath.

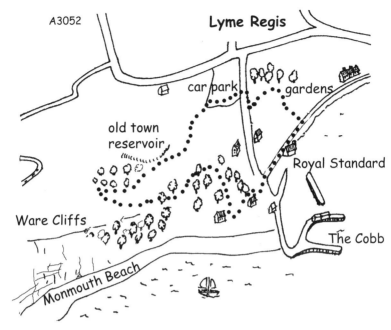

Follow the direction indicated, up the steps and towards the cliffs. The footpath goes up the cliffs and is well signposted. In wet weather it can be muddy and slippery. There is a stream that runs to the left side of the path.

The path passes through woodland and eventually comes to a stile with a built-in dog flap. You are now out of the woods and into a field. Bear left after the stile, and follow the coastal footpath sign. The footpath crosses a stream via a small concrete bridge, and then passes through a gate. Carry on up the hill. The National Trust owns this area of Ware Cliffs. The land here is very unstable, and there are frequent rock falls onto the beach.

The views are stunning; out to the east is Portland Bill, and at night the lighthouse can be seen flashing from its furthest end. To the left of Portland is Chesil Beach, which runs along the coast to the piers of West Bay. Closer still is the distinctive cliff of Golden Cap, with its crowning glory of yellow cretaceous sands – at 191 metres it's the highest point along the whole of the south coast.

The footpath is easy to follow. Continue up the hill. The bank on the right hand side is part of the former cement works reservoir.

Eventually you come to another intersection – take the path ahead and carry on up the hill to a gate, which you go through. If you look down at the Cobb you can see the harbour buildings perched on the wall. These buildings were at one time bonded warehouses, than an isolation hospital, before eventually becoming a sailing club and the aquarium. The harbour itself dates back to the 12th century, though much of the present structure is from the 18th and 19th centuries.

Carry on up the hill, still following the coastal footpath signs, until you come to a junction and another gate. Take the path on the right side up the hill. The coastal footpath route passes through the gate towards the bungalow and out onto the Tarmac road. If you follow the Tarmac track for 10 minutes you will come to Underhill Farm, which is slowly going over the cliffs, and was used as a location during the filming of 'The French Lieutenant's Woman'.

Carry on up the wooded path, which is the final ascent before the drop back into Lyme Regis. At the top of this wooded hill is a perfectly placed bench, where you can regain your breath and enjoy the view.

Continue along the path until reaching a gate; ahead in the distance beyond the town are the cliffs of Black Ven. These are the most unstable cliffs in the area, and the mudflows are the largest in Europe. Many of the finest fossil finds are made at their base.

Start the descent down the hill, with the gorse hedge on your left, to the side of the old reservoir, following the barbed wire fence past the ruins of a pump house. Bear off to the right, and cross over the stream via an earthen bridge, and continue towards the path to the right of the houses.

Follow the sign for Lyme Regis and pass through the gate. The footpath eventually leads out onto a Tarmac drive and then on into Holmbush car park. At the corner of the car park there is a notice board showing the route of the Southwest Way. Keep to the left hand side of the car park, and cross the drainage ditch and over the road to the pavement. Walk down a little way and you will come to the turning for Langmoor Gardens. At one time the garden was wooded, but a landslide in 1962 caused a great deal of damage. Follow the footpath down through the gardens and out onto Marine Parade. Turn right, and you will come back to your starting point at the Royal Standard.

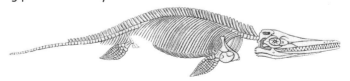

10. LYME REGIS - CHARMOUTH BEACH WALK
Walk time: 1 hour
Distance: 1½ miles
Walking: easy

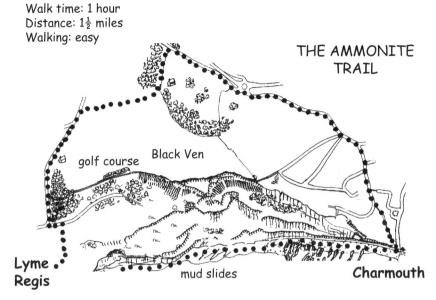

THE AMMONITE TRAIL

golf course   Black Ven

Lyme Regis

mud slides

Charmouth

This walk can only be completed if the tide is out and the state of the tides should be checked. Follow the sea defence pedestrian walk along the seafront of Lyme Regis, going east towards Charmouth; the sea defences and walkway eventually will lead down to the beach.

After crossing a series of groins that jut onto the rock ledges, the cliffs rise up looking like a multi-layered cake. The layers were once the Jurassic sea floor; the nearer to the bottom of the cliffs, the older the period. The rock is called 'Blue Lias' and is particularly important to palaeontologists for the number of fossils contained in it. It is on this section of cliffs that many of Lyme Regis's famous fossils have been found.

The Blue Lias cliffs gradually sink away as one nears the cascading cliffs of Black Ven, the front of which is marked by a snout of rock, mud and debris. These cliffs are almost living, and move and fall with such frequency that 2 photographs taken only ten years apart would hardly look the same. The plateau above the beach is treacherous, with bog and marsh ready to trap anyone. The cliffs are un-climbable as the face gives way at the slightest touch.

On a quiet day, the beach has a variety of sea birds, including most of the gull family and groups of oystercatchers. The rock pools contain shrimps and prawns. Offshore are the marker buoys for crab and

29

lobster pots. This beach is reckoned by local anglers to be the best for fishing, as on a high tide, at night, dogfish, skate and conger come in to feed on the muddy beach.

Along the beach, the old Charmouth cement works is clearly visible; the building now houses the Charmouth Heritage Centre, café and fossil shop. The Heritage Centre has an excellent exhibition about the fossils and rocks of this area of Dorset.

The beach at Charmouth is also of historic interest. Vikings landed here twice, raping, pillaging and other Viking activities, and there is record of a battle in the area. This was also scene of an unsuccessful escape attempt by Charles II after his defeat at the battle of Worcester, while fleeing Cromwell's soldiers.

The car park at Charmouth marks the end of this part of the walk; you can return to Lyme over the cliffs (see the next section) or walk back along the beach (check tide). There is also a bus service that runs through the village of Charmouth, which is another half-mile inland.

CHARMOUTH TO LYME REGIS VIA BLACK VEN AND THE COASTAL FOOTPATH
Walk Time: 1½ hours
Distance: 2½ miles
Walking: A slog up hill

You cannot walk back to Lyme Regis if the tide is in. Always check the time of the tide - you can normally walk from Lyme Regis to Charmouth about an hour either side of low water. If you do get cut off, you can either catch a bus or book a taxi or walk back to Lyme Regis on the coastal footpath. The walk is a slog uphill but is well signed and worth it for the views.

The walk back over the top of Black Ven was once easy but due to intransigence and problems of ownership of land, it does now involve a bit of a trek. Follow the footpath sign, which is immediately on the left after the "Charmouth Heritage Centre". The footpath comes out onto Higher Sea Lane. Turn right and follow the lane up the hill out onto the main road. Turn left up the hill and eventually you will come to a roundabout. Go left up "Fern Hill". A short distance up the hill is the "Fernhill Hotel". The footpath from the road is on the left, on the edge of the woods. The path skirts the edge of the grounds of the hotel and enters the woods. It is a steep ascent and the path emerges from the trees onto the golf course. Cross the links and through the hedge and turn left at the main road. Carry on down this road and follow it when

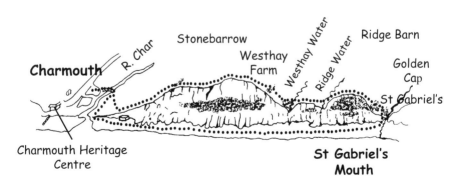

it goes off straight ahead, called Timber hill. Follow this lane down past the Golf Course. Towards the end of the lane, before you reach the main road, there is a track that goes to the left, through a wooden five bar gate out on to the cliffs. Take this track, and shortly on the right take the footpath that goes down hill and crosses the fields back to Lyme Regis.

Footnote
The old footpath followed the cliff edge, which it had done for thousands of years, and had always moved back slightly inland after any loss due to erosion or slippage. The lack of willingness of some members of the golf course has closed the natural route of this footpath. As a result, one of the best views of Black Ven and Lyme Bay has been lost, and the walker is now forced to tramp for a long section by the main road and the distance has been doubled. If you feel strongly over this please write to: Dorset County Council's Rights of Way Officer at Dorchester.DT1 1BR. One day the proper route might re-open.

11. CHARMOUTH TO ST GABRIEL'S CLIFF AND BEACH WALK
Walk time: 2½ hours
Distance: 4 miles
Walking: muddy, hilly; quite tough

This walk is along one of the most scenic parts of the Jurassic coast and is about 4 miles in length. The walk is hard going and involves a few steep ascents and descents but is well marked; if it's too difficult, it's easy to turn round and head back. Allow about 2½ hours for the walk. The coastal path goes through the National Trusts Golden Cap Estate which covers 2,000 acres of farmland, woods, cliff and gorse common, extending 7 miles between Lyme Regis and Eype's Mouth.

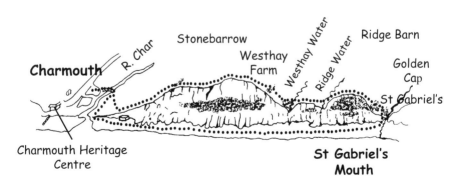

Charmouth — R. Char — Stonebarrow — Westhay Farm — Westhay Water — Ridge Water — Ridge Barn — Golden Cap — St Gabriel's

Charmouth Heritage Centre

St Gabriel's Mouth

The Golden Cap Estate is managed and farmed in a manner that encourages both plant and wildlife. Some of the fields have a traditional hay-cut in late spring, which encourages nesting birds and rare flowers, such as the spotted orchid. Free roaming cows and sheep graze much of the open common land, so dog owners should beware. The grazing helps control the spread of gorse and bracken. The cliffs of the coast yield numerous fossils, from ammonites to dinosaurs. It was due to the uniqueness of the geology that this stretch of coastline was granted World Heritage status.

The cliffs along the coast are very unstable and landslides and rock-falls frequently occur, and the shape of the coastline continually changes. On the beach there are numerous spurs of mud and debris; these can block access along the beach at high water. It is worth asking at the Fossil shop or Heritage Centre that the way is clear to come back along the beach before undertaking this walk. Also ask about the time of high water, as ideally this walk is best done when you can come back at low water.

The start is from Charmouth Beach car park. Charmouth is one of the few places in Dorset where it is normally possible to park close to the beach. On the sea front is the 'Charmouth Heritage Centre', housed on the top floor of a former cement works. Inside, there is a free display about the fossils and coastline of this section of the coast. Below is the world famous 'Charmouth Beach Fossil Shop'. On display at the rear of the shop, in a large glass case, is the huge fossil skull of an Ichthyosaur found in cliffs that this route encompasses. There are also numerous locally found fossils on sale.

Park the car, bike or helicopter in one of the car parks and head towards the River Char and cross the wooden bridge to the eastern bank, and follow the marked footpath that leads up the side of Stonebarrow. I would not advise going too close to the edge of the cliffs. The cliffs are unstable especially in the winter months when there are frequent falls. After about 30 minutes of steep ascent you should reach the top of Stonebarrow. From the summit you can look across to the highest point on the south coast, Golden Cap. (190 metres above sea level). The flat summit is covered in a layer of golden sandstone (greensands), which contrasts with the grey stones and clays of the Jurassic rocks.

The coastal footpath is well signed and goes down from the summit of Stonebarrow, passing Westhay Farm on the left, with its cottage and collection of old barns. The path down can be muddy. Much of the coastal path follows the edge of the cliffs and the route can be seen crossing the field to the right in the distance.

Continue following the coastal footpath and across the wooden bridge that goes over Westhay Water. A stile is soon reached, and you continue to follow the coastal footpath, ascend a steep field and eventually reach another stile. It is worth stopping for a rest and to get your breath back. Try closing your eyes and listen to the sounds of local birds and the whistle of the wind, although sometimes it can be just the sound of powerboats zapping offshore below the cliffs.

The crescent of this hill provides an excellent viewpoint. Behind in the distance is the coastal town of Lyme Regis with the ancient harbour (The Cobb) jutting out into the sea. Above Lyme Regis and to the west is the Undercliff Nature Reserve. The land is heavily wooded and the footpath runs through glades of trees and is almost jungle in appearance. If you turn round and face east there is Golden Cap and tucked behind; to the left is the forested top of Langdon woods. Our path to the beach is at the foot of Golden Cap, just before St Gabriel's.

Proceed along the path, which follows the edge of a huge landslip. At one time this would have been hedges and fields, but as cows and sheep can no longer graze the land it has started to revert to its natural state, and woodland has reclaimed ancient pasture. This raised inland side of the footpath makes this a great place to bird watch, as the footpath is like walking in a tree canopy. Follow the footpath and in the distance, at the foot of Golden Cap, are the few buildings that remain of the ancient village of St Gabriel's.

St Gabriel's
On this walk we do not go as far as St Gabriel's, (but to reach it is only a ten minute walk from the beach footpath). St Gabriel's is one of the many lost villages that dot our landscape. During the medieval period this was a thriving community, although the population quickly declined after the ravages of the Black Death. Today, all that remains are an old farmhouse and a couple of labourers' cottages (now let as holiday accommodation by the National Trust), and the ruins of the medieval church of St Gabriel's. (Each summer a local theatre company puts on a play among the impressive remains of this ancient chapel).

Back on the route, on the right and through the hedge, is a new path that deviates from the coastal footpath and leads down to the beach.

The footpath is signed advising walkers to be wary of the tide times. The beach section of the walk is best done about three hours before or after high water. The footpath down to the beach is muddy and slippery and at the last section, steps have been bolted into the cliff face. There are a total of 78 steps down onto the beach. The descent is impressive and the transformation from country walk onto beach is sudden. One minute the sound of woodland birds and the next the sound of waves crashing onto the shingle beach.

The original steps where on the eastern side of the St Gabriel's stream, but became too dangerous due to slides and the water washing away the bottom of the path. The new steps were opened in 2006 and are the only access point down to the beach between Charmouth and Seatown.

The Beach walk back to Charmouth
Start the beach walk back to Charmouth (west) this section should take about 1 hour. Please do not walk under the cliffs as all those boulders and rocks come down with regularity.

On the beach you can find washed out fossils such as belemnites (bullet shaped fossils) and the curly ammonites. It can be hard going walking on the loose shingle. The best time to walk is at low tide when the hard sand is exposed. The cliffs are impressive and the grey rock is the ancient Jurassic seabed, raised up and eroded by the sea. On the beach you will see people searching for the fossil remains of creatures that lived over 195 million years ago. Look at the shingle recently turned by the tide and you can often find small washed out ammonites.

When you get back to Charmouth, there are two cafes and a pub in the village for sustenance.

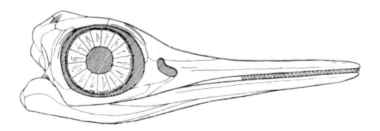

12. SEATOWN, LANGDON HILL AND GOLDEN CAP

Walk time: 1½ -2 hours
Distance: 2½ miles
Walking: hard

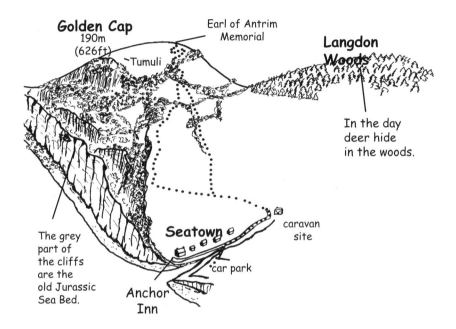

Golden Cap
190m
(626ft)
Tumuli

Earl of Antrim
Memorial

Langdon
Woods

In the day
deer hide
in the woods.

The grey
part of
the cliffs
are the
old Jurassic
Sea Bed.

Seatown

caravan
site

car park

Anchor
Inn

Seatown is a small fishing hamlet on the Dorset coast mid-way between Charmouth and Bridport. To reach Seatown, turn off the A35 at Chideock. Seatown is a mile down the winding, country lane. There is a car park opposite the Anchor Inn Public House.

The footpath to Golden Cap is well marked and runs from the road inland of the Anchor Inn and is easy to follow; there are fields on the right, and cliff and scrub to the left, which offer some slight protection from the wind.

Shortly there is a sign for Langdon Hill, which is the wooded hill to the right of Golden Cap. Our path crosses the stile and up the side of the field to Langdon Hill. To the front of the woods is a second stile and the track that leads off to the top of Golden Cap. The final climb to the summit is sharp and steep and will have even the fittest puffing and panting, but it is worthwhile for you have now conquered the highest cliff on the south coast of England and from now on it's all down hill.

Golden Cap is 190 metres above sea level, the highest cliff on the south coast of England. The name is an apt description of the cliff face, the exposed upper greensand and gualt on the summit to the seaward side produces the characteristic golds and yellows of the Cap. The Golden Cap estate is now owned by the National Trust and covers 1,294 acres. From the summit are some of the best views of West Dorset. To the north is the little village of Morecombelake, exposed and windswept in winter by westerly winds. To the northeast is the forested Langdon Hill. To the west is Charmouth, once the scene of a battle between warring Danish raiders and resident Saxons. Black Ven separates Lyme from Charmouth and is the most unstable of all the local cliffs; no two pictures taken in a decade would look the same, as the cliffs continually slip and move. To the east is the snout of Portland Bill protruding out into Lyme Bay, a home to the navy, prisoners and fishermen. At night you can see the lighthouse flashing its warning to passing ships.

A brief excursion down the western side of Golden Cap will take you past the ruins of St. Gabriel's Church, once the parish church of the lost village of Stanton St. Gabriel. The old coaching road used to run along the coast through Stanton St. Gabriel and on towards Charmouth, and the village drew most of its wealth from passing traffic. When a new road was built, due to the old route falling into the sea, it was one and a half miles further inland. The population of Stanton St. Gabriel declined and the village died.

The church was built in the thirteenth century and was first mentioned by the Bishop of Salisbury in 1240, when it was considered a significant church. By the Middle Ages both the village and its importance had declined and the parish was administrated from Whitchurch Canonicorum. By the end of the eighteenth century the church was no longer used and became derelict. Enterprising fishermen soon found a new use for the church - smuggling. Brandy, silks and tobacco brought from France were rowed ashore on the deserted beaches of St.Gabriel's and stored in the ruins of the church. Ghost stories were spread to deter even the most persistent of revenue men from investigating the strange flashing lights. The smuggled goods were then taken inland along the back roads of the Marshwood Vale. The introduction of stiffer penalties and the building of coastguard cottages at Seatown largely stopped smuggling.

After our brief look at the ruined church of St.Gabriel's we return up to the top of Golden Cap. The route back down to the car park is by following the coastal footpath down to Seatown.

Seatown has always been a small fishing hamlet, though now caters for the tourist industry with caravans and tents. In former times the chief

occupation was netting mackerel from the large shoals that came inshore during the summer. Because of over-fishing, the large shoals have disappeared, though Seatown is still very popular with beach anglers, and good catches of bass, conger and cod have been taken from its shores.

13. SEATOWN, THORNCOMBE BEACON AND EYPE'S MOUTH
Walk time: 2 hours
Distance: 4½ miles
Walking: up and down along the cliffs

Park at the Anchor Inn, Seatown.

Climb up the grassy slope eastwards following the coastal footpath up to the top of Doghouse Hill. Keep to the cliff footpath ignoring all other paths that branch off to the left. Carry on up the hill towards the summit of Thorncombe Beacon. It's a steep climb to the top but you can now follow the footpath down the hill into Eype, and the small river that empties onto the shingle beach.

Follow the narrow lane up the hill and look out for the sign for the footpath on your left, just before a bungalow. Go up this next field, keeping near to the hedge on your right. Cross the stile into the field and walk on up the hill to the opposite corner, where you meet the bridle path.

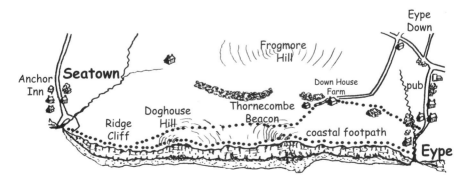

Turn left along it in the direction of "Down House Farm", making for the angle of the hedge, which is close to your left as you approach the farm.

Between the farm buildings turn left and take the track that goes straight on, towards the sea. Ignore the other tracks that branch off to the right.

The footpath bears round left and then right across a field, which slopes down to your left. The footpath keeps to the contour. Walk through the gate in the hedge at the far corner and you will come to a bowl shaped valley that sweeps down to the cliffs. Follow this track, close to the hedge on your right. You then cross a stile into a field past the tumulus (Neolithic burial mound), and with hedge on your right, cross the stile at the far end. The footpath meanders but you are now approaching the landward side of Doghouse Hill. The footpath passes through some rough scrubland, with the land falling steeply on your right. Carry on westwards and you will soon find yourself at the top of a steep-sloping hill, and back to the car park.

14. BURTON BRADSTOCK
Walk time: 1 hour
Distance: 2 miles
Walking: easy, but slippery when wet

The walk starts at the Three Horseshoes Inn, a 17th century building in the centre of the village. Leave in pub behind you and turn left, to follow the mail road for a short distance, crossing the river and passing a shop and tearooms. Then cross the main road to the lane dead ahead, to the right of the garage. Follow the lane up a steep hill through a deep cutting to Burton Cliffs, owned by the National Trust.

Just before you reach the cliffs, turn right by a stone wall and follow the Dorset Coastal Path. Keep well clear of the cliff edge. Some 200 yards on, heading west, there is a signpost pointing to Burton Bradstock, which you ignore and carry on along the well-worn cliff path. There are occasional seats along this part of the path, with wonderful views of Portland to the east and Golden Cap to the west, with Lyme Regis beyond.

The path begins to climb slightly and West Bay's East Cliff comes into sight. The cliff marks the start of Chesil Beach, and is a nesting place for many a jackdaw and gull.

The path descends, and the large caravan park of Burton Freshwater lies below you, with the Mere, and the beach into which the River Bride disappears.

Now there is a steep descent – almost a slide in wet weather, so take care! At the bottom, pick yourself up and climb the stile to take the meadow path heading towards Burton Bradstock. Keep the caravan park to your left. There may be cattle in this field, so you can reflect on the interesting fact that a cowpat can be home to 80 different species of beetles, flies and bugs!

The river on your left was once used for 'retting' (or soaking) flax. Both hemp and flax were once widely grown in the area, to supply local industries in the making of linen, sailcloth, hammocks and netting.

Pass a little bridge over the river and continue along the path with the village church clearly visible to your left. You then come to some buildings, and climb the stile beside a Wessex Water compound. You are among stone and thatch again, passing the old Dove Inn on your right. Back at the 'T' junction next to the garage on the main road, turn left back into the centre of the village, and return to the Three Horseshoes.

Burton Bradstock

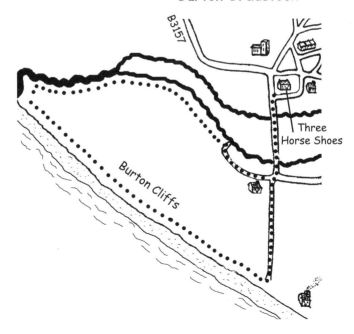

ABBOTSBURY

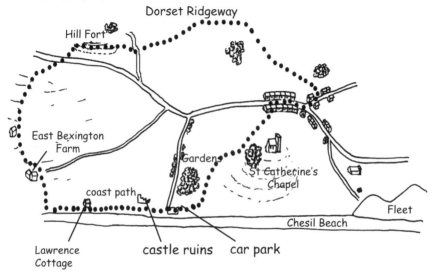

Dorset Ridgeway

Hill Fort

East Bexington Farm

Garden

St Catherine's Chapel

coast path

Fleet

Chesil Beach

Lawrence Cottage

castle ruins

car park

15. ABBOTSBURY CIRCULAR WALK

Walk Time: $3\frac{1}{2}$ hours
Distance: 6 miles
Walking: some steep climbs to the hill fort and St Catherine's Chapel, and can be muddy

Abbotsbury is one of the most attractive villages along the Dorset coast. The estate belongs to the Strangways family; you will not see any lampposts, and any new building is in keeping with the village.

The area around Abbotsbury has been extensively farmed and settled for thousands of years, and many early Neolithic burrows and features dot the landscape. The Romans also came to the area, and traces of a Roman villa have been found in plough debris. The early Church built the monastic settlement that the village is named after. The dissolution and break-up of the religious estates by King Henry XIII resulted in the land and title being passed into the hands of private families.

The village is situated 9 miles from Weymouth and 9 miles from Bridport, on the B3157. Even if you do not do the walk in this book, this is one of the most beautiful roads to drive along in Dorset, with sweeping views of Lyme Bay, Golden Cap, the Chesil Beach and the Isle of Portland, which protrudes into the English Channel.

The starting point for the walk is the car park at the Chesil Beach, past the Sub-Tropical Gardens. The gardens are signposted off the main road on the western side of Abbotsbury. The car park is situated behind the Chesil Beach. In winter it is free to park - a rarity along the Dorset coast where every access seems to be charged at a premium. (Although after reading this they will probably charge!)

Proceed west from the car park, following the rough road that lies on the inland side of the Chesil Beach. To the right are the ruins of Abbotsbury Castle.

The castle was built in 1765 as the summer residence of the Fox-Strangways family, who also had the adjacent sub-tropical gardens constructed. The tender plants flourish due the microclimate, and frosts are rare in this sheltered position. The castle burnt down in 1913 and was never rebuilt. The family own the manor and title of the estate, which includes the right to any shipwreck goods washed up on the beach. Carry along the lane with the Chesil Bank on the left.

The Chesil Bank is 17 miles in length and runs from West Bay in the west to Portland Bill. The action of the waves and the prevailing southwest winds grade the pebbles of the beach, with the smallest deposited in the west and the large boulders in the east at Portland. It was said that smugglers landing spoil on a foggy night could tell their position by looking at the size of the shingle. The Chesil has some attractive plants such as sea campion, yellow horned poppy and sea kale. There have been many shipwrecks on this beach during southwest storms, and even now coins and bits of debris can be found after a big storm. The beach also attracts numerous anglers even in the depths of winter.

As you walk along the road, on the left and right are abandoned WW2 gun emplacements. The Fleet farther along was the testing zone for the famous bouncing bombs used by the RAF in WW2 to breach the dams of Ruhr. The story was turned into the film, 'The Dambusters'.

Walk on past Castle Cottages and the private drive to Lawrence Cottage. A little further along on the right is the waymark stone for the circular walk and hill fort. Leave the Coastal path and follow the path up the hill which runs to the side of the field up to East Bexington Farm. The path curves around the back of the farm, past the old tyres, and across the field at right angles towards another cottage. On the other side of hedge is the start of the steep ascent to Abbotsbury hill fort. The path can be very muddy. At the end of the ascent there is a signpost and a dry stone wall. Go right, and follow the wall until eventually it reaches the main road, which you cross, then follow the track up onto the banks of Abbotsbury hill fort.

The hill fort is one of many that dot the high points of Dorset, built by the Durotrige tribe and pre-dating the Roman invasion of 43 AD. It covers about ten acres of land, and is highly unusual because of its triangular shape. When it was in use it would have had a wooden palisade on top of the earth works, and would been a very striking feature, dominating the coast and the ancient track-way that runs along the top of the Dorset down land. Archaeologists have never properly excavated the fort, but the traces of eleven hut circles have been found inside its ramparts. More is known about the nearby hill fort of Maiden Castle at Dorchester, which was attacked by the Roman legions, and its defenders slaughtered.

Follow the footpath that goes to the trig point (the concrete pillar, used by surveyors to calculate height, and map the surrounding features). On the ordnance survey map this is marked with the small blue triangle (grid ref 556 866). Walk along towards the beacon post.

From the summit of the fort are some of the best views in Dorset. To the east you can see the column of the Hardy's Monument. (This has nothing to do with Hardy the novelist; it was built to honour Hardy the naval officer, whom Nelson wished to kiss on his deathbed after the battle of Trafalgar). Portland Bill is to the right, and below is Abbotsbury, with its church and collection of medieval buildings, and the impressive St Catherine's Chapel on the conical-shaped hill. Follow the edge of the escarpment for about a mile due east and look for the sign directing you down towards the village. As it descends it goes past and through some old stone quarries.

The track eventually comes out onto a lane that leads to the high street. Turn right at the end of the lane and walk down to the village centre. If you are tired you can rest at one of the many tearooms, or stop at the Ilchester Arms pub.

The walk back to the car is about a mile from the centre of the village. Go west along the high street away from the pub and past the old school; on the left is a small store selling newspapers and food, and the lane back to the car park is signposted to the right of the shop.

Follow this track, which is flat and level, all the way back to the car park. For the more energetic, you can divert up to the top of Chapel Hill to St Catherine's Chapel, which is usually open to the public, and has some wonderful views. After about 3 hours you will arrive back at your car.

16. PORTESHAM TO HARDY'S MONUMENT
Walk time: 2 hours
Distance: 3½ miles
Walking: two hills to climb

Blackdown Hill

Hardy's Monument

Hell Stone

Black Down Barn

Black Down Farm

Portesham

St Peter's

B3175

Old Quarry Dinosaur scultpture

Portesham is an attractive village on the B3157 that runs from Bridport to Weymouth. This is an ideal walk for a morning or afternoon and ambled at a moderate rate should last about 2 hours. There are two hills but the route is easy to follow and the landscape and views are panoramic.

If you are coming along the main road then you will need to turn off into the village; alternatively you can come by the coastal bus that runs along the Dorset Jurassic coast. Park outside the parish church of St Peter's. The church dates back to the 12th century, although much of the building is from the 15th century.

Walk up Front Street past the local post office and some attractive old cottages, and continue up the road. On the right, after a short distance, is a finger-signed bridle way for our destination - Hardy's Monument.

The bridle way runs to the back of the houses, and is also a farm track; at the end of this short stretch you pass through a metal gate, with the end of the houses on your left. This is the steep part of the ascent.

43

Follow the farm track and bridle way up the hill, with the stone wall on the left. This must be an old drovers trail as the bridle way is worn and sunk into the hill; hawthorn and scrub mark the sides of the route. It's worth stopping as you go up the hill and looking at the surrounding landscape.

The chalk downs of this part of Dorset are pockmarked with remains of early Neolithic, Iron and Bronze Age settlements. A short distance to the west there are numerous burial chambers (tumulus). There is one chamber, which was restored in the nineteenth century, called "Hell Stones". The stones were once the inner burial chamber of a Neolithic long barrow built 5,000 years ago. A lot of the early burial sites crowd the high points of the landscape. Not far from Portesham are the ancient hill forts of Maiden Castle and Abbotsbury Castle, both of which were started about 3000 BC.

Enough of the history... continue panting up the hill. At the crest, on the right, is a duck pond. Pass this, and follow the dry stone wall up and round to the right. Carry on following the dry stone wall, which is in very good condition and looks as if it was only recently re-laid. Go through the gate at the top of the field and start the descent down the bridle path. On top of the hill ahead is the first view of the distinct outline of Hardy's Monument, perched on the summit of the hill.

To me, Hardy's Monument has always had the appearance of an early industrial chimney and I always expect to see black smoke billowing out of its top. I suppose if you wanted a monument in the early nineteenth century it was either a statue (costly), or you engaged a tower/chimney builder. The monument choice was limited.

The bridle way goes down the hill and through the abandoned farmyard called "Black Down Barn". The buildings are in a forlorn state but the architecture of the old barn on the right seems very old, with defensive arrow-firing points set into the wall. At the bottom of the valley and past the farm buildings, go through the gate and turn left. There is a sign at the bottom of the path that goes up through the woods - 'Portesham $\frac{3}{4}$ mile, West Bexington $4\frac{1}{2}$ miles and Hardy's Monument $\frac{1}{2}$ mile'. Follow the sign for Hardy's Monument.

The footpath goes up through the coniferous woods. Plantations of conifer always seem strangely silent, with few birds. The plantations were established in 1964 by the Forestry Commission and were restricted to land up to the 700ft contour. More recently, as the conifer woods mature and are felled, the Commission has started replanting with mixed species of trees.

Keep following the track up through the woods and do not deviate from it. Hardy's Monument is at the top of the hill. Eventually, you come out of the woods onto the open gorse and common area at the bottom of the monument. Much of the area is scarred with old quarry working. There is a stone way marker on the left of the path stating that Osmington Mills is eleven miles away, which is interesting if you live at Osmington Mills.

You have arrived at Hardy's Monument. The tower stands on top of the Blackdown (or Blagdon) Hill, 780ft above sea level. The panoramic view is one of the best in Dorset. To the south and southeast can be seen the end of Lyme Bay. The Chesil Beach with the Fleet tucked behind it. Portland Bill juts out into the sea. To the east is the Roman town of Dorchester and the ancient hill fort of Maiden Castle, and far off into the distance the white cliffs of the Isle of Wight.

Thomas Masterman Hardy
He was the second son of Joseph Hardy, and was born at Kingston Russell in 1769. He spent his boyhood living at Portesham House, which was the centre of the family estate. He enrolled in the Royal Navy at the age of 12, and in a long career he eventually became the captain of Nelson's flagship HMS Victory. He fought at the battle of Trafalgar, where Admiral Nelson defeated the combined Napoleonic French and Spanish fleets. It was to Hardy that Nelson, lying mortally wounded at the end of the battle, uttered his most famous dying words, "Kiss me Hardy." It is also thought he could have said "Kismet, Hardy." (Kismet is an Arabic for word for "fate"). I am sure if I had been shot in the shoulder by a musket ball and mortally wounded my language would not have been as controlled, and the thought of kissing Hardy, no matter how attractive, would have been the last thing on my mind...enough!

Thomas Masterman Hardy survived the battle and went on to become First Sea Lord, and later the Governor of Greenwich Hospital. He died 1839 at the age of 70. The 70ft high monument was erected in his memory in 1844. Inside, the tower has 120 steps to the top, opening out onto a viewing platform, which sadly is not open to the public.

Hardy's Monument has no connection to the famous Dorset author Thomas Hardy, who died in Dorchester in 1928. Hardy wrote numerous novels such as "The Mayor of Casterbridge," which have a backdrop of nineteenth century rural Dorset. In 1998, a group of Japanese enthusiasts of the famous writer flew to England and with great reverence laid flowers at the foot of the monument to the author. Dorset folk were too polite to tell them the bad news that they had the wrong monument!

At the monument, proceed over to the display panels and there is a second memorial, which is a seat dedicated to William Digby Oswald, who died of his wounds at the Battle of The Somme, 16th July 1916. He had an adventurous life fighting in the Boer War, after which he returned to Dorset, married a Weymouth girl and settled in Rhodesia, gold mining. At the start of WW1 he rejoined the army, fought at Mons, Ypres, and was eventually killed by shells falling short from his own guns at Mons.

The footpath back down runs to the right of the display panels, with the old quarry workings on the left. The gravel pit was excavated during WW2 to provide hard standing at Weymouth for the vast numbers of military vehicles and stores prior to the D-Day landings.

Take the footpath down till it joins a track that skirts just inside the eastern edge (Weymouth side) of the woods. Follow the winding track all the way down till you come back to the ruined farm buildings of "Black Down Barn". These are the ruined farm buildings passed on the way up, at the bottom of the valley. Follow and stay on the bridle way up the hill, and carry on to Portesham Farm. The outbuildings look wrecked but the farm is still working. The surrounding trees by the farmhouse are tilted away from the prevailing southwest winds. A short distance from the farm the bridle way crosses over a cattle grid and onto the Tarmac farm driveway. Follow the driveway down the hill ahead towards Portesham. On the left there are old quarry workings, and in front of an information panel is a splendid dinosaur made out of agricultural machinery welded together. In the distance, on the top of the hill above Abbotsbury, is St Catherine's Chapel.

The farm track eventually comes out onto the road. Follow the road, turn right, and this brings you back to Portesham.

St. Catherine's Chapel

46

17. MOONFLEET
Walk time: 2 hours
Distance: 3 miles
Walking: mostly quite flat, muddy in parts, and along the lane part of
the way, so some care is needed

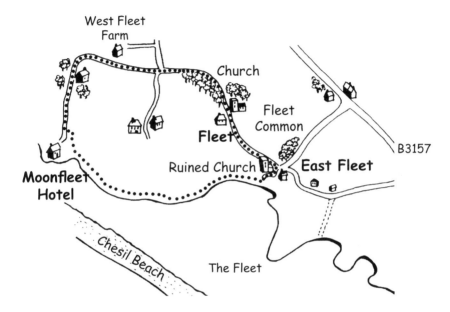

The tiny hamlet of East Fleet was made famous in John Meade Falkner's
novel Moonfleet. Little remains of the original village, which was all but
obliterated by the great storm of November 23rd, 1824, when waves
tossed a 90-ton sloop, the Ebenezer, onto the top of the Chesil Bank,
and a tidal wave crashed through the tiny village, destroying cottages
and most of the church. A new church was built further inland five years
later; many years afterwards, the remains of the old church
were restored.

It still contains the 17th century memorial brasses of the Mohun family,
and their family vault lies beneath the stone floor, complete with its
secret smugglers' passage leading away to the Fleet. There is also a
small plaque to the memory of Meade Falkner.

Getting there – take the B3157 coast road that runs between Bridport
and Weymouth. Turn towards the sea at Chickerell on to a road marked
'Fleet ½'. Drive along this road for about a mile. Passing the church
and some houses on the right the road bends slightly to the left, and

47

just past this there are some car parking spaces under the trees on the right. Park here, and walk back along the road in the direction you arrived, passing the new church, which was completed in 1829. You will come to some cottages on the right, the road you drove down curves away to the left, and there is a track beside the cottages. Take the track, going through the gate. Follow the track along beside the churchyard wall, ignoring the branch to the left.

At the end of the track turn right and follow the path with the field fence on your left. Go over the stile, through some bushes along a narrow path until you reach another grassy track, and here turn left. Follow the track, with the water of the Fleet to your left.

The Fleet is a narrow salt-water lake that separates the Chesil Beach from the mainland. It starts on the outskirts of Weymouth, in Portland Harbour, and runs all along the coast as far as Abbotsbury to the west. The water is quite shallow, and often full of seaweed. It supports large numbers of fish, and a tremendous variety of birds and wildlife.

Carry along the track until you reach a fence; keep this on your right, and follow the path, with the water to your left. Where the fence ends, follow the edge of the field, and the path curves gently away from the Fleet. Ignore the stile into the woods on the left. Shortly after this, you will come to a gate on your left.

Go through the gate into the field, and follow the track across the field, bearing right towards a metal gate. Once through this gate, you will be on the narrow road; to the left is the way to Moonfleet Hotel. Turn right, uphill and away from the coast. Follow the road, passing a farm and through some woods. Where the road divides into three, carry straight on the middle branch, and you will shortly arrive back at your start point.

Chesil Bank and the Fleet from Portland

18. PORTLAND BILL WALK
Walk time: 1 - 1½ hours
Distance: 3 miles
Walking: easy, mostly level

Much of Portland seen from the road is ugly. The landscape is scarred by ex-Ministry of Defence buildings, designed with the inspiration of a low-achieving hamster, and fences everywhere, mostly in a state of decrepit rust. The landscape is scarred with holes and shattered rocks from the numerous quarries... but this a brilliant walk and one full of surprises and fantastic views of the Dorset coast. The walk takes just over the hour and is full of interesting things to see (apart from the rusty old fence that surrounds Southwell business centre). It should be

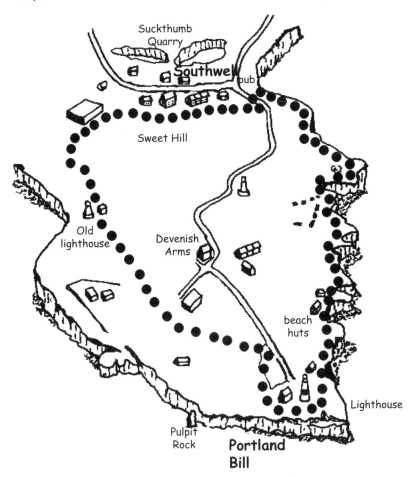

impossible to get lost on this walk and due to its short route and lack of any high hills is ideal for children.

Portland Bill juts out into the English Channel and dominates the Dorset coast, as quiet a few sunken ships can testify to, who over the centuries have managed to sail into it!

Start the walk from the car park at the tip of Portland Bill by the lighthouse. The footpath starts at the top land end of the car park and goes up the grassy downland towards the old lighthouse and ex-Coastguard watch on the hill. The path passes to the right of the old lighthouse with 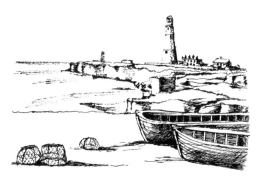 Coastguard watch house and sea on the left. From the top of the hill it's worth pausing and having a look at the surroundings. Ahead is Weymouth and the Chesil Beach which stretches all the way down to West Bay, about 17 miles away. In the distance to the west are the cliffs of Lyme Regis and East Devon. Behind is Portland Bill lighthouse and out to sea are normally lots of boats and ships. Along to the east is another ex-lighthouse, which is now a bird observatory, and in the east are the cliffs of Lulworth, Kimmeridge and the Purbeck Hills. This has to be one of the most spectacular views in Dorset.

We will carry on... ahead is a large ex-Admiralty building which now houses Southwell Business park. The footpath carries on towards this building, which has a fence surrounding. The footpath we need is on the right and runs to the side of the fence. A small hedge runs to the other side of the fence, which gives shelter from the wind.

Follow the path that runs to side of the ugly fence, although there is an edge of the field which also seems to be used, till it comes out by the entrance to Southwell Industrial Park and onto a Tarmac road. Follow the road down the hill, past the bungalows, for about 50 meters and on the right is a finger sign for the footpath and track leading up a slight hill. On the left is another stile footpath signed. Take the path on the left over the stile with the finger sign pointing to "Warsend Cove, $\frac{1}{2}$ mile". Over to the left behind the village of Southwell is Suckthumb Quarry.

Portland Stone

Many of London's finest buildings are built from Portland Stone. Sir Christopher Wren used the stone to rebuild St Paul's Cathedral, after the Great Fire of 1666. The Cobb at Lyme Regis was also repaired in the 18th century using Portland Stone.

The stone was originally extracted from cliffs on the east coast using the natural fractures and gullies in the rock. The coastline is littered with the debris from these early workings. The local quarrymen and fishermen have a superstition about saying the word "rabbit" and will go out of their way not to include the word in any conversation. The mention of the word "rabbit" will cause disaster to strike. There is logic as to why this normally harmless animal is hated on Portland. Rabbit diggings would cause the face of a quarry to become unstable and collapse. So when walking the path do not refer to the "grey fury things" to a native Portlander.

The quarry at Suckthumb is still being worked and used for the extraction of the Portland limestone. Behind the quarry is one of the old Portland forts, now converted into a prison. Portland has one of the highest prison/borstal populations in the country. In the eighteenth century prisoners built the harbour breakwaters at Portland Harbour. The harbour was created to provide a safe anchorage for the Channel fleet, and at one time prisoners were kept on hulks prior to transportation to Australia. In the 1990's the Royal Navy closed the Naval Base down and left an island littered with redundant housing, buildings and a harbour. Slowly the island is recovering from this economic bombshell.

The track comes out onto the main road, turn left and about 60 meters on the left is the sign for the footpath, which is just to the side of the building with a gantry protruding from it.

The footpath runs down and past the old quarry workings and joins up with the coastal footpath. Turn right and follow the footpath. The path is sunk below and away from the road and all you can hear is the sound of the sea and birds. All along the route are the old quarry workings with lots of rocks and discard. Along the edge by the cliffs are the old gantries once used to load the stone onto boats.

The path comes out onto the grassy common area near Portland lighthouse and lots, and lots of garden sheds. They do look ugly each in uniform creosote brown. They must be very brave owners as the wind here in winter and even in summer blows across from the Atlantic. Portland Lighthouse is open to the public. The building was erected in 1908 replacing the other which is now used as a bird observatory.

Portland is surrounded by dangerous waters. The Shambles is a shallow bank of sand and shingle that has claimed many ships, while off-shore is the Race, an area of bubbling waves created by the clash of two tidal currents meeting. To avoid getting caught up in the Race many boats take the inshore passage which seems very close to the cliff edge at the Bill.

The whole area is owned by the Crown Estates and it is a shame that the huts are not in any other colour, but perhaps Prince Charles has shares in Creosote. Follow the path out onto the open common and grassland that leads back to the car park. I have to admit when doing this book I didn't think that Portland could offer such an interesting walk. The Ministry of Defence and Quarry companies really should clean up some of the mess they have made. In both cases they have taken a great deal from the land but given very little back. It wouldn't take a lot to improve the place - a good start would be removing the barbed wire and fences, and rip down some of the ugly derelict buildings.

19. OSMINGTON MILLS & RINGSTEAD BAY
Walk time: 2½ hours
Distance: 5 miles
Walking: mostly easy

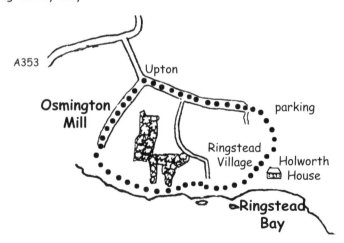

This 5-mile walk is a good way to explore the cliff tops of the Dorset coast without needing to be very fit to do it. Allow just over 2 hours for the walk, but more if bringing younger children for whom this walk should be possible. There are one or two small ups and downs along the way, with just the one, long steady climb towards the end.

You can park at the National Trust car park, high above Ringstead Bay, not far from South Down Farm. Get there by turning off the Weymouth to Wareham road about a mile east of Osmington village. The narrow road passes through Upton, heads towards Ringstead village, but at the point where you head to the right to the sea, carry straight on and reach the parking area ½ mile later.

Take some time to admire the stunning view, and then continue away from the entrance. The sea is to your right and you should continue along the gravel track through the car park, until the parking area ends 200 yards later. Climb the stile, then carry along the track for about 100 yards to reach another stile and gate.

Cross once more and arrive at a junction another 100 yards later, where the turn to the left should be ignored. Just 30 yards later ignore a turn to the right, this time to Marren, Seafields and Helwarden; follow the bend to the right. This takes you towards "Coast Path ¼", ignoring the route ahead to West Lulworth in the process, and past Sea Barn Farm instead.

To the right are views of Weymouth and Portland in the distance, and a valley below that you keep on your right as the track descends. In 70 yards, fork to the right along the track marked "Ringstead Beach", and continue a now steeper descent. This quickly eases and at this point you come across one of Dorset's most charming churches.

The short detour to the left to admire the delightful, wooden chapel of St. Catherine's-by-the-Sea is a must. This humble place of worship is constructed entirely of wood, including all the pews, alter, lectern, candlesticks and collecting boxes. Its history dates back to Dr. Linklater, former Prebendary of St. Paul's Cathedral, who bought Holworth House a few yards to the east of the church in 1887. When he died in 1915, his wife lived in the house for 11 more years, when she sold the property and used some of the proceeds to have the chapel built in memory of her husband. The full story of the chapel can be found on a plaque inside. Outside in the graveyard there are views across the huge undercliffs at White Nothe, with their mix of chalk rock faces and lush greenery. The cliffs above rise in places to 500 feet; below them the undercliff extends to an area of 115 acres, so it is not surprising that animals as large as deer can be found in these very quiet and fairly inaccessible conditions.

Leave the church by the gate and return to the route by continuing downhill. You soon reach a gate to a cottage, which you pass to the left of and follow the clearly signposted route to "Ringstead ¾". Passing between scrub to the left, behind which the land drops to the sea over Burning Cliff, and the cottage to the right, continue downhill for about

70 yards. Pass another sign, cross a stile, then through some scrub, using the steps on the way. Continue ahead for 100 yards or so, ignoring the turn to the right to South Down Farm on the way. About 50 yards beyond this, you emerge from the scrub, and continue ahead, between a fence on the left and a hedge on the right, keeping to a clear track all the time. This improves in quality and continues for ¼ mile to reach a caravan park on the edge of Ringstead village.

Not far beyond is a small shop, and the track ends immediately after it. Turn left here, as signposted to Osmington Mills and reach the beach about 100 yards later. Turn right and follow a wide gravel track, keeping the sea to the left and houses to the right. After about 100 yards, the track ends, and you go 15 yards diagonally left at this point, past a marker stone and into the scrub beyond.

Beyond the undergrowth, a clear path leads ahead, still with the sea to the left, but with a field to the right. The path heads through a reed bed, which is unusual, being slightly elevated area. This soon ends and leads instead into a small wood, through which you first head downhill, then cross a stream, before climbing uphill up some steps. A short detour to the left at the bottom of the dip brings you to another good area of pebbled beach.

Out of the trees once more, continue along a clear path that reaches a stile 200 yards later. Cross this and pass a wartime pillbox. A fence remains on your right as you walk the ½ mile to Osmington Mills, passing a total of four fields on your right on the way, with the sea always to the left. About half way along this section, look down into the sea to spot the decaying remains of a stranded ship, now put to use as a resting place for the cormorants.

Just before reaching Osmington Mills, head downhill over a stile and descend a flight of steps, then pass through some scrub, before climbing another stile. The village is now straight ahead and you head for a stile downhill and slightly to the right, beyond which a short detour can be taken to the Smugglers Inn, the roof of which is clearly visible ahead. Back on the route, turn right before the village and head uphill along a well-worn grassy path through a marshy field, which aims for a chalet site in some trees. Keep a fence about 30 yards away to the left as you climb, then cross over a stile on the far side of the field and enter the chalet site.

Continue uphill along a clear track to the right of some of the chalets, then cross another track and continue the ascent. You leave the site at the top of the hill, passing through a gap in the fence that brings you out on to another track. A footpath sign directs you to the left, but almost immediately afterwards the route forks and you head right and start to climb again. This is the inferior of the two paths and comes to a stile about 200 yards later. Cross this and continue uphill, all the time getting better and better views to the left over the valley.

When the climb finishes, continue along the level, keeping the hill to the right and the valley to the left. Eventually you reach a gate and stile that brings you out onto a Tarmac road heading towards the little hamlet of Upton. This lane soon ends at a junction with the road you took to the car park. Turn right here and go up the minor road signposted to Ringstead. The climb is long and steady, but the views to the left across the valley are lovely. Ignore the footpath down to the hamlet, continue to climb, then 50 yards later ignore the right hand turn to Ringstead as well. Instead, carry on towards the National Trust car park along the minor road, and in ½ mile you are back at the car. Before you leave, it's worth reading the fascinating information boards in the car park, which give some facts about the history and natural history of Ringstead.

20. HOLWORTH TO LULWORTH
Walk time: 3 to 4 hours
Distance: 8 miles
Walking: hard going, with stiff climbs and descents

The chalk cliffs between Lulworth Cove and Holworth are some of the most spectacular in Dorset, and make for some wonderful views. This is, however, quite a tough walk, and you really need to be fairly fit, and allow plenty of time in order to enjoy it.

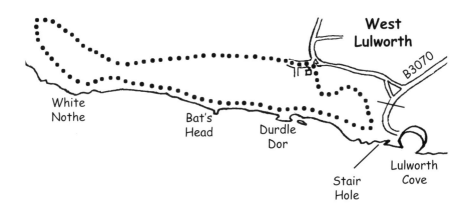

The walk begins at Lulworth Cove (West Lulworth), where there is a large car park, and the fee for parking includes admission to the Heritage Centre. Head to the furthest end of the car park from Lulworth Cove, and over a stile onto a wide chalk path that leads to Durdle Door. Immediately over the stile, turn right and follow the fence on your right. The signs are for Durdle Door caravan park and the youth hostel. After 200 yards you will come to another signpost, continue ahead towards the camp, still keeping the fence on your right.

When the first field ends, cross a stile, and go ahead across another field, the fence still to your right. You start to climb, and head for the stile on the skyline. Once over this, carry on uphill through two more fields to Durdle Door caravan park. Go right, and follow the main road through the site. You pass the site shop, go downhill and then climb again, leaving the park as you do.

Just before reaching the road, the track forks, and you go left, away from the road and towards Newlands Farm. Go right by the farmhouse, and the Tarmac turns to gravel. At this point, turn left at another fork and head uphill away from the farm. You reach a sigh post to Ringstead and White Nothe, and carry on along the track, which ends 75 yards later.

Here go through a gate into a field and keep the fence on your right. At the far right hand corner of the field, pass between a fence on the left on the left and the one still on the right. Head diagonally right as directed by another signpost, and pass a solitary marker post in the middle of the field.

At the end of the field you will come to a stile, which you cross, and then follow the route ahead towards Ringstead. This part of the walk is easy to follow as you pass through five fields, keeping the fence to your right, and the sea to your left, climbing gently. In the fifth field there are three sculpted snails mounted in the bank on the right, and there is also a navigational obelisk in an adjoining field.

Not long after passing the snails, the trail swings to the right. Carry on to the next fence, passing a memorial stone to Dorset author Llewellyn Powys. Just beyond the route swings to the left, and continues in the original westerly direction.

About 100 yards further on you head downhill and reach a junction of tracks at a gate. Turn left and follow the clearly signed route to the coastal path, which will lead you back to the car park.

21. TYNEHAM AND THE ARMY RANGES

Walk time: 4 hours
Distance: 7½ miles
Walking: several hard climbs

Every walk in this book can boast a variety of views, but if there were a prize for the walk with the best views, then this route would surely win it. At times, not only can you see the sea close by, but also views of Dorset that extend into other neighbouring counties. So wait for a clear day before tackling this wonderful journey.

Timing is important for another reason. The walk passes through the Royal Armoured Corps tank gunnery ranges for much of the way, so access is restricted to those days when the ranges are open to walkers. In general, this is at weekends and the school holidays. Roadside signs will warn you well in advance as to whether you have chosen a good day or not.

You start at the free car park and viewpoint just above Great Wood, high on the Purbeck ridge. To get to this parking area, turn off the Wareham bypass at the turning to Kimmeridge. Follow this road for about three miles until the long ascent by the lovely Creech Grange house. This wooded climb ends quite suddenly at a spot where the views inland open up. Almost immediately on your left you will then see the car park, itself with spectacular views out to sea.

Start the walk by turning your back on the sea. Head towards the road, keeping to the right hand side of the car park. By a flagpole is a way marker pointing along the ridge way path. Immediately right of this is another marker directing you to "Steeple 1". Follow this clear track that heads downhill.

Within 100 yards it bends right, then continues its descent to a minor road. Turn left here and continue downhill, although keep well in to the verge, as the road is fairly narrow and well used in summer. As you head along the road, the small village of Steeple gets ever nearer. However, you do not reach the village. Instead, at the point where the road takes a sharp bend to the left, near a sign to Lutton Gate firing point, go straight ahead along a track to Steeple Leaze Farm.

This right of way is signed to "Kimmeridge $1\frac{1}{4}$" and passes between fields, before dropping down to the farm in the dip ahead. Passing through the farmyard you pick up a narrower path that continues ahead, passing the farmhouse on the left. Once over a stream, climb along this tree-lined track. The cover ends in 50 yards and emerges in a grassy area, beyond which is scrub. Go straight ahead to follow a fairly indistinct path next to the hedge on the left, leaving the bridle way that continues diagonally right uphill.

The path you take narrows and gets muddier through the scrub. When the bushes and trees end, you find yourself about 10 yards away from the track you were on before, which is still to your right. Turn left here and climb steeply, turning your back on the bridle way as you ascend. The climb is hard but quite short and in about 75 yards brings you to a stile, which gives access to a field beyond.

It is worthwhile stopping for a moment to admire the countryside you are leaving behind you. Follow the footpath arrow and keep a mixture of wall, fence and hedge on your left to climb through the field. Suddenly, a whole new selection of views opens up, including Corfe Castle some distance away to the left, and the hill-fort at Flower's Barrow to the right. On a clear day, the coastal landmarks of Clavell's Tower and Portland Bill stand out.

At the end of the field is a stile, which you cross, then continue through the next field for 30 yards to another stile. Cross this, and follow a stone sign to Kimmeridge Bay and the church. Passing through some quite thick gorse you head downhill to reach another stone sign in the rough grass. Turn right here and head towards the bay, taking care down what is at first a steep descent. However, as soon as the rough grass ends, you enter a field and the ground is level once more.

Cross this field and a further two more, making for the clear gaps in the hedges ahead all the time. The final exit is just to the left of a small wood, this gateway giving access to one final field before you reach a minor road just short of Kimmeridge Bay.

Turn right here and head off towards Dorset's first "nodding donkey", an oil extraction facility opened in 1959 and still in use. You follow the road for about 100 yards until it veers to the right. Cross at this point to a cliff-top path and a coast path sign. Turn right and walk parallel to the road along the path, keeping the impressive bay to your left. Look out for the distinctive Kimmeridge Ledges that lead out from the cliffs into the bay, at times exposed by a low tide.

In 150 yards you pass the oil station, with an interesting information board about the area. Soon you enter the ranges, passing more information boards on the way. You must keep within the yellow posts at all times whilst walking in the ranges. However, the marking of the clear trail is excellent.

The route to Tyneham starts as a wide, clear track, passing farmland to the right and the bay to the left. This level section is short lived and in a mile or so, just over the second cattle grid, fences border your route either side and you start a long climb. As compensation, the views rapidly improve as you gain height, with the cliff formations at nearby Gad Cliff catching the eye in particular.

The wide path with fences on both sides ends at a stile, which you cross, before continuing uphill. Once again between the yellow posts, you swing sharp right about 100 yards later, follow a level section for 50 yards, then swing left and climb steeply for another 50 yards or so. Once the worst of this climb ends, you follow a contour of the hill on your right across open ground, keeping the sea on the left. About 200 yards later the path appears to fork, but continue along the lower route, still within the markers and as shown by the footpath sign.

You are aiming for a small stone ruin on the skyline, which you pass. Cross a stile near to it, then turn left and follow the cliff-top path immediately above the impressive rock formations at Gad Cliff, which you saw earlier. All the way along the ridge the views are good, with Tyneham valley becoming more obvious to your right as you progress. About half way along the ridge a short cut can be taken down to the village of Tyneham. Keep within the yellow posts as you descend. However, if you have the stamina, it is much better to follow the ridge down into Worbarrow Bay, which you reach about $1\frac{1}{2}$ miles later This stunning bay is well worth exploring, with the Iron Age hill-fort of

Flower's Barrow perched high above the next cliff to the west along the coast.

Head inland along a gravel track, signposted to Tyneham. The mile or so it takes to get to the village is a magical ramble passing through a rich variety of scenery. To the left there is often gorse, or later a lovely wood. To the right, the grasslands, occasionally interrupted with the wrecks of tanks and other target practice.

When the path ends, you are almost at Tyneham village. To reach this romantic spot, turn left, walk through the parking area and in 100 yards or so reach the village.
Tyneham is one of Dorset's truly unique features; a village evacuated in 1943 to allow the armed forces much needed firing ranges, as the Allies prepared for the invasion of Europe and the D-Day landings. However, the temporary evacuation became permanent, leaving an entire parish of 3000 acres devoid of people.

The village, which is being renovated in many places, is well worth exploring. Take time to investigate the school, built in 1860 and now an information centre, the church, and even the old telephone kiosk.

The walk continues by taking the track, which goes to the right of the church, and then swings left, then across open ground towards the ridge ahead. Keep within the yellow markers. The ascent is easy at first but becomes more difficult when the track goes to the right about half way up.

At the summit of the ridge there are some lovely views inland, which remain to your left once you have turned right and followed route towards Whiteways car park. The road remains behind the fence on your left and yellow markers continue to the right as you walk the mile along the ridge to the car park.

Once at the car park, continue straight ahead and pick up another marker-bordered path on the far side. You are back next to the road, which remains the case for the next mile until you descend to cross the Tyneham lane. A stile on the other side of the lane leads to another mile section of bordered path, which in turn comes out at a road junction within sight of the car park where you left your car. Cross the final section of open ground and take a last chance to enjoy this most scenic route of the whole selection.

22. PURBECK - KIMMERIDGE & KINGSTON

Walk time: 5 hours
Distance: 8½ miles
Walking: some steep climbs; children and dogs should be kept under control near the sea, as landslips occur along this part of the coastal path. This is a long walk, but perfect for taking a picnic.

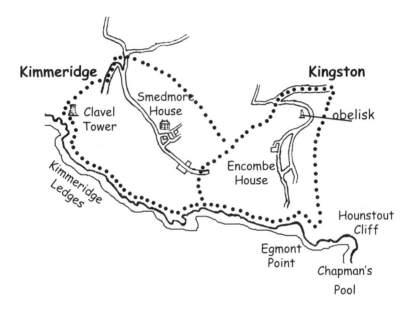

Kingston and Kimmeridge both have large country houses and are only a few miles apart on the Isle of Purbeck. However, there are some significant differences between the two villages, as you will discover on this exhilarating walk.

The hilltop village of Kingston boasts a massive Victorian Church. It's a landmark for miles around, perched high on the Purbeck Ridge. Built by the 3rd Earl of Eldon, whose descendants' family seat at Encombe House is passed during this walk, the church is dedicated to St. Stephen. The nearby St. Nicholas' Church in Kimmeridge is one of Dorset's most simple churches, nestling in a hollow close to the sea. Its single bell epitomises the charm of this delightful place of worship. The owners of nearby Smedmore House preferred to build other landmarks; their offering is Clavell's Tower, a folly built in 1831 high above Kimmeridge Bay.

The walk starts from the Encombe Estate free car park, just west of Kingston village. From the entrance, turn left and follow the minor road, with trees at first on either side. In about 200 yards the trees end, giving lovely views to the right. Whilst the familiar shape of Corfe Castle stands out, the stunning hills either side of the monument are just as impressive.

About ½ a mile from the car park, you reach another parking area with information boards. Turn left here and pass between two stone pillars. Continue ahead for 10 yards and into a field from which a clear bridle way leads away towards Swyre Head a mile away. Climb and swing right through the first field to pass into another. A wood should now be immediately to your right.

On your left is Encombe House. This 18th century mansion has one of the most secluded sites of any country house in Dorset. Long and low, with its south front looking out over a pair of lakes, it lies at the bottom of the Golden Bowl, a long valley between the hills and the sea. It was the home of philanthropist William Morton Pitt. He was followed by John Scott, the first Earl of Eldon, an early 19th century Chancellor. Eldon Seat is the stone seat where he used to rest with his dog, Pincher, to whom there is a memorial stone. The Earl of Eldon also erected the forty-foot Egyptian-style obelisk in 1835 to honour his brother, Sir William Scott who had been created Baron Stowell. Sir William drafted the world's first basic maritime laws and the stone appropriately acts as a landmark for Channel shipping.

Carry on along the high ground and eventually left to climb to the Bronze Age round barrow that helps to make Swyre Head the highest point in Purbeck. From the top you can see both Encombe and Smedmore Houses, much of the Isle of Purbeck and on a clear day, the Isle of Portland.

From Swyre Head, pass to the left of the triangulation point and follow the bridle way to Kimmeridge. (A shorter route is possible by descending from Swyre Head to Rope Lake Head on the coast). For the next 1½ miles keep the fence, wall and hedge to the left and follow the ridge, with the sea to your left.

The descent becomes steeper just before a minor road, where you turn left. Fifty yards later at a T-junction, go straight ahead and follow the signposted footpath to "Kimmeridge ¼". The descent takes you to the left of St Nicholas' Church into the village.

It is possible to take a fairly long detour from the village at this point, to visit Smedmore House, which is open on Wednesday afternoons in the summer (follow the signs from the church). The house was built in 1620 by Sir William Clavell, and has been owned continuously by either the Clavells or Mansels since then. The estate gained its name from its first owner, a Norman by the name of Smedmore, who probably took his name from the surrounding countryside, as it means "smooth moor".

Back to the main walk; go through the village passing the cafe and post office on your left, then turn right in about 100 yards, immediately after the last cottage on the right. Take the marked footpath across a field and leave via a double stile and bridge. Over the bridge, turn left and follow the hedge on the left through three fields. You reach a minor road, where you should turn left towards a large parking area.

Turn right at the car park, cross the grass and aim for the low cliff-top, which you should follow towards the nature reserve centre and huts on the shoreline. At the end of the first car park, pass through some scrub to a second grassy area, then turn right 50 yards later and descend carefully to the quay and information centre. Cross a minor road and follow the signposted Coast Path route to climb steeply to Clavell's Tower.

The views from the tower across Kimmeridge Bay to the Army Ranges are stunning. Continue east along the coast path, taking care with any landslip areas and steep drops, often made worse after heavy rain. This 3 mile, undulating section of the Coast Path enjoys views over the Kimmeridge Ledges. These fingers of rock stretch out into the sea and are often well exposed at low tide. Inland, the most obvious landmark is Swyre Head. The final 400 feet ascent of Houns-tout is as hard as any in Dorset, but is very rewarding. A thoughtfully placed bench provides a good resting place.

At Houns-tout turn left and follow the ridge inland for a mile or so. Pass through several fields, keeping a wall on the right and Encombe House to the left. It was here during a fire at the house in 1811 that the first Lord Eldon buried the Great Seal of England to keep it safe from the flames. Unfortunately, the exact spot he chose was not marked and it took some time before the seal was recovered. Not wishing to lose it again, the Earl of Eldon became the longest serving Lord Chancellor, only giving up office in 1827 after 25 years.

At the end of the fields you enter some trees. About 200 yards into the trees, pass Nursery Tea Rooms, and take care at a staggered junction. Keep going (mostly) straight ahead, until you find the clear footpath to "Kingston $\frac{1}{2}$". Follow this track until just before the minor road, where you turn left through a small gap in the hedge to find your car park.

23. BALLARD DOWN, STUDLAND AND OLD HARRY
Walk time: 2 hours
Distance: 3½ miles
Walking: mostly easy

The walk is the starting point of both the Jurassic Coast World Heritage Site and the start of the South West Way which is about 600 miles in length and circles the southwest peninsular from Poole to Minehead in Somerset.

Studland was once the haunt of smugglers and pirates. Ballard Down is a chalk ridge that separates the Isle of Purbeck from Dorset's eastern heath lands. This walk is ideal for keen birdwatchers as the unblemished convex walls of chalk attract many sea birds.

The walk starts with one steep ascent up the top of Ballard Down (500ft) and the complete circuit should take about two hours. A pleasant walk on a warm summers, day but can be windswept and cold in winter. The walk has great views of Poole Harbour, The Needles and Swanage, and Studland's famous nudist beach - although on the day I did this walk, it was mid-winter and even the Polar bears were wearing overcoats.

Park the car at a lay-by in the small hamlet of Woodhouse (B3351). This is the back road that connects Corfe Castle to Studland. The lay-by,

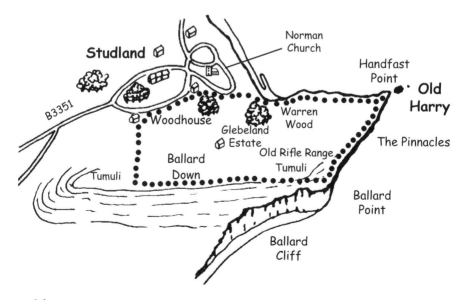

which is not made up, is marked with a large advert for the Bankes Arms Hotel and is convenient for the footpath that is about 20 yards away in the west. The path is signed "Swanage via Ballard Down." Ballard Down is the large hill in front.

Follow the footpath down through the woods and out onto a field; there is a small thatched cottage on the left, a typical west county style. Go down the hill to the gate, which is positioned at the bottom of the small valley, and follow the footpath, which now goes up through the centre of the field towards a stile. Go over the stile and onto the down. Follow the steps and keep on ascending, eventually coming out onto the crest that is about 500 feet above sea level.

That is the hard bit done. The track to the cliffs is on the left and runs along the crest of Ballard Down. Follow the wide track all the way to the "trig point" (a trig point is a triangulation point used for fixing and surveying the landscape and at one time was maintained by the Ordnance Survey). They are the concrete pillars, which you find on many high spots that provided an excellent survey position.

At the trig point (0400 8103) follow the footpath that bears to the right and through the gate and towards the cliff edge. This is the coastal footpath that runs from Poole all the way round the coasts of Dorset, Devon, Cornwall and Somerset. A wide variety of wild flowers grow along the cliff-tops above Ballard Point. There are lots of cormorants which can be seen on the rocks and fishing off shore. Follow the coastal footpath towards Poole past Ballard Point with its pinnacles of eroded chalk and onto the chalk stacks of Old Harry and the stump of Old Harry's Wife. At Old Harry there is an information board.

The name Old Harry is a synonym for the Devil and the gap between the land and the stack is called St Lucas's Leap. The original Old Harry's Wife crumbled into the waves in 1896. The land around the foreshore of this area is called "Old Nick's Ground." This is definitely not a place to camp on Halloween night.

The erosion of the soft chalk by the action of the sea forms the stacks; caves are formed which widen and eventually collapse leaving an isolated stack of chalk. These make great nesting places for seabirds.

Follow the coastal footpath past Old Harry and into the woods. The track from Studland to

Old Harry passes through a wood where ramsomes, red campions and bluebells grow and ivy arches overhead. The track is well used and easy to follow. Eventually the track comes out onto a road (with some public toilets on the right). Turn left up the road and continue into the small village of Studland.

En route, you pass Manor Farm on the left and on the right is an old Norman Church of "St Nicholas of Myra," (patron saint of sailors) and in the centre of the small grass area outside the church is replica of a carved Saxon Cross. There is even a "Saxon Tractor" in the brick shed on the left with metal wheels! The church graveyard contains an interesting burial, that of Sergeant William Lawrence of the 40th Foot Regiment. He was a soldier who fought during the Napoleonic Spanish War and also fought at Waterloo, eventually marrying a French woman and came to Studland to run a local pub. He died in 1896.

Shortly after the cross there is footpath which signs for Woodhouse. The path runs parallel to the road and eventually takes you back to the car and start of the walk.

Further information...

Another great way to see the Jurassic coast is from the top of a double decker bus. The views are wonderful – many cannot be seen from a car.

The Jurassic Coast Bus service is ideal for walkers who want to walk part of the coast path and return by bus.

The service (COASTLINX53) connects Exeter, Sidford, Beer, Seaton, Lyme Regis, Charmouth, Bridport, Abbotsbury, Weymouth, Wool, Wareham and Poole (summer service). It runs every two hours, including a Sunday service, with new low floor buses, and unlimited travel on a £5 pound day ticket (2006 prices). The majority of the buses used on this route are double deckers, though some services may be single decker, so if you want to be sure of the views, it's best to check first.

For information and timetables telephone Traveline on 0870 608 2608.

There is also an excellent web site, giving information about the whole of the National Heritage site, including details for the bus service.

Go to www.jurassiccoast.com